ASSASSINATIONS
that
Shook
America

ASSASSINATIONS
that
Shook America

Edmund Lindop

FRANKLIN WATTS
NEW YORK / CHICAGO / LONDON / TORONTO / SYDNEY

Photographs copyright ©: Archive Photos: pp. 1, 2 top, 4 (Dean), 11 top, 14 top (AFP); North Wind Picture Archives, Alfred, ME: pp. 2 bottom, 3, 5, 6, 7 bottom; The Bettmann Archive: p. 7 top; Library of Congress: p. 8; UPI/Bettmann Newsphotos: pp. 9,16 top; Historical Pictures Service, Chicago: p. 10 top; AP/Wide World Photos: pp. 10 bottom, 12, 13, 14 bottom, 15, 16 center & bottom; John F. Kennedy Library, Boston, MA: p. 11 bottom.

Library of Congress Cataloging-in-Publication Data

Lindop, Edmund.
Assassinations that shook America / Edmund Lindop.
p.   cm.
Includes bibliographical references and index.
Summary: Examines the causes and effects of the assassination of
seven prominent Americans, including the four presidents killed in
office and such significant political leaders as Martin Luther King
and Robert Kennedy.
ISBN 0-531-11049-4
1. Assassination—United States—History—Juvenile literature.
2. Presidents—United States—Assassination—Juvenile literature.
[1. Assassination—History.   2. Presidents—Assassination.]
I. Title.
E179.L58   1992
364.1'524'0973—dc20   92-15082 CIP AC

CONTENTS

*This book is dedicated to Mark Feldman,
former student, researcher, typist, and
cherished friend*

INTRODUCTION

The term *assassination*—meaning murder for political reasons—is from the twelfth-century *hashashin*, the name of a bloodthirsty Muslim sect that disposed of its political enemies by slaughtering them. Throughout history many important world figures were assassinated either by individual murderers or by conspiracies. Among the most prominent victims were the Roman ruler Julius Caesar; Jean Paul Marat, the French revolutionary; Russia's Czar Alexander II and the Communist agitator Leon Trotsky; Mohandas K. Gandhi, India's famous religious and political leader; Anwar El-Sadat, the Egyptian president and first Muslim head of state to conclude a peaceful agreement with Israel; and Indira Gandhi and her son Rajiv, both of whom served as Indian prime ministers in the latter part of this century. The assassination of another political leader, Archduke Francis Ferdinand of Austria-Hungary, was the spark that ignited World War I.

In some parts of the world, especially in countries accustomed to autocratic regimes, one of the most common ways to change the government is to stage a sudden military coup; the head of state is then murdered, imprisoned, or forced into exile. The United States, with its democratic procedures and well-established system of peaceful elections, has been spared military coups, but it has not been free of assassinations. Four American presidents—Abraham Lincoln, James A. Garfield, William McKinley, and John F. Kennedy—were slain while in office. Other presidents, including Andrew Jackson, Harry Truman, Richard Nixon, Gerald Ford, and Ronald Reagan, were the targets of unsuccessful assassination attempts. After his presidency, Theodore Roosevelt was shot but not killed, while campaigning in 1912 for another term in the White House. Two decades later, Franklin D. Roosevelt was president-elect when he narrowly missed a bullet intended for him that instead murdered Anton Cermak, mayor of Chicago.

This book discusses the four presidents who died at the hands of assassins. It tells about their backgrounds, accomplishments, and shortcomings, as well as the circumstances surrounding their untimely deaths. Then it explores in detail the changes that the United States experienced after the former vice presidents assumed in midterm the highest office in the land. To some extent, the new presidents tried to follow the plans and policies laid down by their predecessors; in other instances, they embarked on paths scarcely or not at all traveled by the men they succeeded in the White House.

Other prominent American political leaders besides presidents have been assassinated. This book also discusses three of them: Huey Long, Martin Luther King, Jr., and Robert F. Kennedy. Each of these men made important contributions, and at the time of his death each had millions of devoted followers.

Assassinations are cruel, unexpected acts that often have widespread repercussions. Those told about in this book shook the lives of many Americans who had placed their trust in leaders who were suddenly, brutally struck down. Countless people mourned the passing of their fallen heroes, and the course of history never was the same after these leaders were gone.

CHAPTER ONE

ABRAHAM LINCOLN

His Death Unleashes a Torrent of Troubles

The jubilant crowd in front of the White House eagerly pressed forward. Light from the gas lamps on Pennsylvania Avenue was dim, and some of the shrubs and flowers on the lawn were trampled as frenzied people jostled for positions where they might see and hear the president. Between the stirring marches played by the Marine band, the crowd joyfully chanted, "Lincoln! Lincoln!" Hundreds of Washington citizens demanded an appearance from the tall, homely man who had championed the Union cause through four hellish years of the worst kind of war that their country could fight—a war in which Americans killed and wounded huge numbers of other Americans.

It was April 11, 1865, two days after General Robert E. Lee had surrendered his Confederate army to the Union general, Ulysses S. Grant, at Appomattox Courthouse in Virginia. Sporadic fighting would drag on for another month, but the collapse of Lee's forces was the dagger that struck the fatal blow to the heart of the Confederacy. The end of the long, tragic war was now clearly in sight, and this was a night for celebration in the nation's capital and throughout the North.

Finally, a French window in the White House was flung open, and the curtains were drawn back. Abraham Lincoln stepped forward and, acknowledging the wildly cheering crowd, waved both hands over his head. He smiled warmly, but the deep-cut lines on his forehead, the dark shadows under his eyes, and the chalky complexion of his face suggested that this was a man who had suffered a terrible ordeal. Leading the nation through the Civil War had taken an enormous toll on the beleaguered president. Again and again, he had been assailed by those who called him "beast" and "tyrant" for prosecuting the war too aggressively, and by others who labeled him "coward" and "fool" because he was unable to bring the hostilities to a swift, successful conclusion. No one wanted peace more than Lincoln did, but not at the price of forsaking the Union.

When the happy throng on the White House lawn finally grew quiet, the president put on his metal-rimmed glasses and began reading in his high-pitched voice from a brief speech he had jotted down on a scrap of paper. He expressed his sincere gratitude that the war was nearly over and soon there would be no new battlefield deaths to mourn. But most of his speech dealt with the uncertainties that lay ahead. He stressed that the restoration, or reconstruction, of the Union would be a formidable task that called for great wisdom and patience.

These sober remarks were not what the celebrating listeners wanted to hear, but they gave the president another rousing cheer when he finished speaking. Two men in the crowd, however, did not raise their voices in the deafening chorus of hurrahs. John Wilkes Booth, his dark eyes flashing with fury, turned to his friend Lewis Paine and said softly, "That's the last speech he will ever make."[1] Then the two men quickly slipped out of the crowd.

After Lincoln's short speech, Senator James Harlan of

Iowa addressed the gathering. When he asked how the defeated Confederates should be treated, many in the audience screamed, "Hang them!" Startled by this vengeful outburst, Harlan suggested that the president might show compassion for the Southerners and pardon most of them for taking up arms against the United States. "Never!" shouted angry men and women, who were determined that the South must be punished severely.

Lincoln understood why many people were demanding that the Confederates be treated harshly for the rebellion they had spawned. There were good reasons for this vindictive attitude. The war had been enormously expensive, draining the resources of a nation poised on the threshold of great industrial growth. More important, the Union dead numbered about 360,000, and the wounded totaled more than 275,000. The Confederates lost about 258,000 men, and at least another 100,000 were wounded. (This was the costliest war in terms of casualties ever waged by Americans, surpassing even World War II, in which about 405,000 members of the armed forces died in battle or of war-related injuries.)

The president, however, had a different point of view from those who wanted vengeful peace terms imposed on the conquered South. He maintained that the Southerners had never actually seceded from the Union. Certainly they had tried to break away, but the United States government had not formally recognized their independence, and the Confederates' rebellion had been laid to rest on the battlefield. The healing process, Lincoln believed, should now move forward swiftly and smoothly. As soon as possible and without rancor or revenge, the vanquished states should be permitted to function again as integral parts of the United States.

How the eleven states of the Confederacy should be dealt with raised several difficult questions. Should their fate be determined mainly by executive orders issued by the president or by laws that Congress passed? How would the

United States government enforce a program of reform on a conquered people? Could it even impose such a program if the Southern states had all the rights of other states? What would happen to the nearly 4 million black slaves freed as a result of the war? How would they find food and shelter now that the plantation system had been destroyed? Should they be granted suffrage (the right to vote) and other civil rights immediately, or should they be kept for a time in some status between full citizenship and servitude? And who should determine their status, the national government or the Southern states?

The political future of the South had been of concern to Lincoln almost from the time the war began, and he had spoken of it to Congress as early as 1861. By the middle of 1863, the Union armies had liberated Tennessee and large parts of Louisiana and Arkansas. Lincoln then began to lay the groundwork for a reconstruction policy that could survive even if he were no longer in office after the 1864 presidential election.

The president announced his program in the Proclamation of Amnesty and Reconstruction, issued on December 8, 1863. In this proclamation he proposed to readmit Confederate states to the Union when, in each state, 10 percent of the men who had voted in 1860 signed a loyalty oath. He also promised to grant a general amnesty (pardon) to all Southerners who would take an oath of allegiance to the United States, except high-ranking officers in the Confederate government and armed forces. In regard to the former slaves, the proclamation was less specific. President Lincoln said that the reconstructed states must acknowledge the freedom of blacks, and he urged that the small number of literate freedmen and those who had served in the Union army be permitted to vote. Beyond that, he seemed willing to let white Southerners work out the details of the blacks' transition from bondage to citizenship.

Lincoln had given much thought to the problems of the blacks after the war, but he failed to find any satisfactory solutions. He worried that the former slaves would not be able to fend for themselves without any education or visible means of support in an economy stripped of the plantations on which they had previously worked. Fearing that most freed blacks could not make a decent living in the United States, the president even considered the impractical idea that they should be sent back to Africa and to the under-developed Caribbean countries. Lincoln also was dubious about giving the vote to freedmen who could not read or write. This was a concern shared by many other Northerners; at that time only six Union states extended the franchise to all black men.

The president's lenient policy toward the South was opposed by the so-called Radical Republicans, who had much support in Congress. They did not believe that the restoration of state governments should be based on loyalty oaths administered to only 10 percent of the white male population. This was a ridiculously small proportion of the population, the Radicals charged, since during the entire Civil War at least 10 percent of the men in every Southern state had remained loyal to the Union. Nor could the Radicals agree to granting amnesty to nearly all Confederates. Furthermore, they asserted that Lincoln had extended his executive powers far beyond their constitutional limits. The Radicals insisted that Congress alone had the authority to initiate policies to reconstruct the Union.

In July 1864, almost a year before the war ended, the Radical Republicans pushed through Congress the Wade-Davis Bill. It required that in each Southern state a *majority* of all white males must take the loyalty oath before that state could be readmitted to the Union. It also excluded from voting and officeholding any person "who has held or exercised any office, civil or military, State or Confederate, under the rebel usurpation [seizure of power] or who has voluntarily borne arms against the United States."[2] In other words, the only white Southerners who would be allowed to vote or hold office were those who had been such strong

Union supporters that they had refused to fight in the Confederate armies.

The Wade-Davis Bill passed in Congress only a few months before the 1864 presidential election in which Lincoln was bidding for a second term in the White House. He greatly needed support from the Radical Republicans to win reelection, so the president wanted to avoid making his action on the Wade-Davis Bill a major campaign issue. His response was a pocket veto, a device which allowed the bill to die because the president had failed to sign it in the last ten days of the congressional session.

The authors of the Wade-Davis Bill were furious with Lincoln. They issued a stinging reply, blaming Lincoln for abusing the legislative power of the national government. The Radical Republicans warned Lincoln that ". . . if he wishes our support, he must confine himself to his Executive duties—to obey and execute, not make the laws—to suppress armed rebellion by arms, and leave political organization to Congress."[3]

After his reelection, Lincoln pressed on with his reconstruction plans. When Congress convened in December 1864, Louisiana became the test case. Its citizens had followed the president's recommendations for reorganizing their state government. More than 10 percent of the white males in Louisiana had taken the prescribed loyalty oath and chosen delegates to a convention that outlawed slavery (but denied blacks the vote and established a segregated public school system). Louisiana also had held elections of officers to serve in Congress and the state government. President Lincoln approved of the steps taken in Louisiana as the best that could be expected from a former slave state, and he urged other Southern states to take similar action.

The following February, Senator Lyman Trumbull of Illinois proposed a congressional resolution to accept the new Louisiana delegation to Congress. However, Senator Charles Sumner of Massachusetts, a leading Radical Republican, vigorously opposed the resolution and Louisiana's request for statehood. Although Trumbull's resolution had the strong support of President Lincoln and congressional moderates, Sumner used various maneuvers to prevent it from coming to a vote in the Senate. As the end of the congressional session neared, important appropriations bills were being stalled by Sumner's tactics to delay a vote on Trumbull's resolution. The resolution was dropped.

On another front Lincoln's reconstruction policies met with more success. The president firmly believed that slavery must be abolished forever in the United States by a constitutional amendment. When this amendment was first proposed in April 1864—at a time when the Confederate states had no representation in Congress—it was approved by the Senate, but it failed to receive the required two-thirds vote in the House. The amendment was introduced again in January 1865 and passed this time in both houses, but a switch of only three votes in the House of Representatives again would have blocked approval. President Lincoln strongly persuaded the states to ratify this amendment, and it was finally adopted, after his death, in December 1865.

Lincoln's attitude of tolerance and charity toward the South was the centerpiece of his famous Second Inaugural Address, delivered on March 4, 1865. In immortal words that have been woven into the fabric of American democracy, he appealed to the people to put vengeance behind them:

> *With malice toward none; with charity for all; with firmness in the right, as God gives us to see the right, let us strive on to finish the work we are in; to bind up the nation's wounds; to care for him who shall have borne the battle, and for his widow, and his orphan—to do all which may achieve and cherish a just, and a lasting peace, among ourselves, and with all nations.* [4]

When Lincoln met with his cabinet on the morning of April 14, 1865, he told the group what he had dreamed the preceding night. He said it was the same dream that had occurred before nearly every important event during the war. Lincoln explained that in this dream he "seemed to be in some . . . vessel, and that he was moving with great rapidity towards an indefinite shore."[5] The cabinet members agreed that the president's dream probably foretold the surrender of the last remnants of the Confederate forces; they had been expecting such news for several days. Such, however, was not the case. Instead, the strange dream might have appeared as an omen of something dreadful that would happen to Lincoln within hours.

That evening President and Mrs. Lincoln planned to attend a play, *Our American Cousin*, at Ford's Theater. As usual, they would be accompanied by only a single guard, in spite of the fact that Lincoln knew he had long been a target of potential assassins. Even before Lincoln became president, while he was traveling from his home in Springfield, Illinois, to Washington, D.C., for his first-term inauguration, his aides had learned of a plot to murder him when his train reached Baltimore. A private coach was hastily summoned, and the president-elect, his face almost covered by a pulled-down hat and scarf, secretly switched trains at Philadelphia for the last lap of his trip to the capital.

At the White House, Lincoln kept in one of the pigeonholes in his desk a bulky envelope that contained information about eighty threats on his life. But the president seldom took any special precautions to protect himself; he seemed fatalistic about assassination attempts. "I do not consider that I have ever accomplished anything without God," he once said, "and if it is His will that I must die by the hand of an assassin, I must be resigned. I must do my duty as I see it, and leave the rest to God."[6]

When he met Harriet Beecher Stowe, the author of *Uncle Tom's Cabin*, Lincoln revealed a premonition of his untimely death. "Whichever way the war ends," he told her, "I have the impression that I shall not last long after it is over."[7]

Word leaked out that General and Mrs. Grant would be the Lincolns' guests in the presidential box at Ford's Theater. Mrs. Grant, however, declined the invitation, explaining that she and her husband would be out of town visiting their sons at a boarding school. So the Lincolns invited Clara Harris, the daughter of the New York Senator Ira Harris, and Major Henry Rathbone, her fiancé, to accompany them to the theater.

The presidential party arrived late at Ford's; the play had already begun. When they saw Lincoln entering his box, the actors stopped and the orchestra burst into "Hail to the Chief." The audience applauded warmly, and then the president sat down in his rocker and put his wife's hand in his. The play resumed, and a short time later Lincoln's lone bodyguard left his post in front of the presidential box and slipped away to a bar.

At about 10:15 P.M., the actor John Wilkes Booth, who had frequently appeared in plays at Ford's and knew the theater well, opened the unguarded door to Lincoln's box. In one hand he carried a pistol, which he aimed at the president's head. In the other he held the dagger that he had planned to use in attacking Grant.

As the audience roared in laughter at a funny line in the play, a loud shot rang out from the president's box. The bullet split in two on impact, one piece stopping in the middle of Lincoln's brain and the other continuing through the brain to the bone of his right eye socket. Major Rathbone lunged at Booth, who stabbed him ferociously in the arm.

Then the assailant leapt from the box to the stage below, tangling his right foot on a flag as he jumped. In a bloodcurdling voice, Booth screamed, "Sic semper tyrannis!" (This expression, the state motto of Virginia, means, "Thus be it ever to tyrants.") His leg broken in the fall, Booth hobbled offstage and behind the theater mounted a horse on which he escaped.

The president's limp body was carried across the street

to a boardinghouse. Early the following morning, Lincoln passed away without ever regaining consciousness.

As the president lay dying, word spread through the shocked capital that other high government officials had also been slain. Although this rumor was unfounded, it was true that the conspirators had plotted the assassinations of four of the nation's most important leaders. The list of potential victims had included, besides Lincoln, General Grant, Vice President Andrew Johnson, and Secretary of State William Seward.

Another untrue rumor was that the conspirators were carrying out orders dictated by the Confederate government. Their ringleader was neither a soldier nor a spy. Instead, he was a well-known actor who had a fanatical attachment to the Confederate cause. John Wilkes Booth was determined to avenge the South's crushing defeat, and he had the deluded notion that history would honor him and the other assassins as immortal heroes for the daring deeds they were pledged to perform.

Booth gathered around him a small band of devoted followers and convinced them that the North would be humbled and gravely wounded if Lincoln and the other "tyrants" were put to death. George Atzerodt was assigned to murder the vice president, and Lewis Paine had the task of killing the secretary of state. David Herold was to go with Paine to Seward's home and later help both Paine and Booth escape. Booth reserved for himself the act of assassinating both Lincoln and Grant, presuming that Grant would be with the president at Ford's Theater. The plans of the conspirators were drawn up in a Washington boardinghouse run by Mary Surratt. (Although Mrs. Surratt knew about the conspiracy, historians are uncertain whether she played a role in carrying it out.)

Atzerodt registered for a hotel room directly above the room in which Vice President Johnson was living. He deposited a loaded pistol under his pillow and several knives under his sheet and then sauntered off to a bar. Atzerodt knew he was supposed to kill the vice president at about the same time that Booth was assassinating Lincoln. But, apprehensive about his mission, he drank heavily, and shortly before the moment when he was to commit his dastardly act, he lost his nerve. Drunk, Atzerodt staggered from the hotel and fled into the street.

That night Secretary of State Seward was in bed at home, recuperating from a painful carriage accident and wearing a leather-covered iron brace around his neck and jaw. Paine and Herold went on horseback to the cabinet member's house, and then Paine alone walked to the front door. Pretending to be a messenger carrying medicine for Seward from his doctor, Paine was admitted into the house and rushed up the stairs. When Seward's son tried to intercept him, Paine fractured the young man's skull with a blow from his pistol. Then, pouncing on the bed, he slashed Seward several times with a knife. As he hurried from the house, Paine thought the secretary of state was dying, but the iron brace around Seward's neck and jaw probably had saved his life. (Seward recovered and lived until 1872.)

Booth and Herold made their way south to a farm near Bowling Green, Virginia. They were hiding in a tobacco barn when federal troops tracked them down. Herold surrendered, but Booth held out as the soldiers set fire to the barn. Whether one of the soldiers shot Booth or Booth shot himself is uncertain, but the stricken actor was carried out of the barn still conscious. Not at all remorseful for the horrendous crime he had committed, the dying Booth murmured, "Tell my mother—I died—for my country. I thought I did for the best."[8]

Atzerodt, Paine, Herold, and Mrs. Surratt were tried by a military commission, found guilty, and hanged. Four other defendants, including Dr. Samuel Mudd, who had done little more than set Booth's broken leg, were given prison sentences.

Booth had killed the one man who might have provided the brilliant mind and strong, steady leadership needed so urgently at this crucial time in American history. Soon after Andrew Johnson assumed the presidency, the problems of reconstructing a war-torn nation became immense and led to deep, ugly rifts, not only between the victorious North and prostrate South but also between the president and Congress.

In some ways Lincoln and Johnson had similar backgrounds. Both had been born in the South of poor rural families. Neither had the opportunity for much formal schooling, but both were ambitious and painstakingly acquired an education. Before entering politics, Lincoln worked as a clerk in a general store and Johnson was a village tailor. All through their lives, in spite of scathing criticism and endless abuse, Lincoln and Johnson shared the same unyielding devotion to the Union.

When the Civil War began, Johnson was a senator from Tennessee. He struggled unsuccessfully to keep Tennessee in the Union; with its secession, he broke with his home state and became the only Southern senator to spurn the Confederacy and retain his seat in the Senate. For this courageous stand he was condemned back home and called a traitor to the South; his life and the lives of his family were threatened; he was hanged in effigy. But in the North he was hailed as a crusading hero.

In March 1862, after parts of Tennessee had been freed from rebel control, President Lincoln appointed Johnson military governor of the state and ordered him to reestablish federal authority there. Governor Johnson moved forcefully to rid the state of Confederate influence, dismissing officeholders he suspected were disloyal, closing down anti-Union newspapers, and seizing the railroads and guarding them from possible sabotage. The stalwart governor remained steadfastly in the capital city of Nashville, even though several times it almost was captured by Confederate forces.

When the presidential election of 1864 drew near and Lincoln's chance of winning a second term seemed in doubt, the Republicans were eager to form an alliance with the

War Democrats in the North and Midwest who had remained loyal to the federal government. So, for this one election they called themselves the Union party and nominated Andrew Johnson, a War Democrat, to run as the vice presidential candidate on the ticket with Lincoln. They did this even though Johnson was a Southerner, had owned a few slaves, and did not switch his party membership to the Republicans. But he was strongly committed to the Union cause and could help Lincoln gain the votes of many War Democrats; these were sufficient reasons for the Republican leaders to make him their vice presidential nominee.

The Lincoln-Johnson ticket won the election, but the new vice president embarrassed his political mentors at his inauguration. Recovering from a bout with typhoid fever, Johnson felt weak and wobbly when he entered the stuffy Senate chamber for the ceremony. He had already consumed some liquor to fortify himself, and he added a few more shots while he was waiting to be sworn in. When he was called on to speak, he slurred his words badly and gave a rambling, incoherent speech with many references to his humble origins and his hatred of the planter aristocrats in the South. Fortunately, his bumbling remarks were overshadowed that day by Lincoln's eloquent inaugural address calling for "malice toward none" and "charity for all."

The day after he became president, Johnson declared, "Treason is a crime, and the crime must be punished. Treason must be made infamous, and traitors must be impoverished."[9] He issued a proclamation accusing the Confederate president, Jefferson Davis, of having planned the assassination of Lincoln, and the U.S. government offered $100,000 as a reward for his capture.

Some of the Radical Republicans were secretly pleased to have a new president in the White House. "Mr. Johnson, I thank God that you are here," said Senator Benjamin Wade of Ohio. "Lincoln had too much of the milk of human kindness to deal with these damned rebels. Now they will be dealt with according to their deserts."[10]

Soon, however, the Radicals discovered that Johnson's reconstruction plan was quite similar to Lincoln's. On May 29, 1865, the president announced that he was granting pardons and returning property to nearly all Southerners who would now take an oath of allegiance. Excluded from this general amnesty were high civil and military leaders of the Confederacy, who had to apply to the president personally for individual pardons. The owners of property worth twenty thousand dollars or more also had to apply for presidential pardons; this provision was aimed at Johnson's enemies, the Southern planters.

Johnson's plan called for the Southerners to convoke state constitutional conventions, which were required to abolish slavery, nullify the ordinance of secession, and repudiate (refuse to pay) the Confederate and state war debts. Significantly, Johnson specified that only white voters loyal to the Union could take part in the constitutional conventions, and these conventions would determine the qualifications of voters in each state. This meant, in effect, that blacks could be denied the vote and that new state governments almost certainly would be controlled by whites alone.

During the summer of 1865, while Congress was not in session, Johnson granted pardons to many former Confederate leaders, and a number of Southern states fulfilled his requirements for readmission to the Union. When Congress convened in December, representatives from eight reconstructed states demanded to be seated. The identities of some of these elected senators and congressmen shocked both Radical and moderate Republicans. Among them were nine Southern generals or colonels, six cabinet officers, fifty-eight Confederate congressmen, and Alexander Stephens of Georgia, who had served as the vice president of the Confederacy.

The appalled Republicans had a majority in Congress, and they denied admission to all these senators and representatives elected in the South. They also condemned Johnson's requirements for the restoration of Southern states, claiming that they were too lenient toward the whites and failed to protect the blacks' civil rights. Then Congress appointed a joint committee made up of members from both houses to draw up another reconstruction program.

Meanwhile, there was mounting evidence that many Southerners already were trying to revive some of the worst features of prewar white supremacy. Southern legislatures began passing laws, known as Black Codes, that were designed to control the former slaves politically, economically, and socially. Under these laws blacks could not vote, sue in court, serve on juries, testify against whites, own weapons, or send their children to integrated schools. In most states freedmen without employment could be seized and hired out to white bosses, and in some states blacks could work only as field hands or house servants.

Fights and riots between blacks and whites broke out in various places in the South. In Memphis, a fight started between police and former black Union soldiers. After six blacks and two policemen had been shot, the police went on a rampage in black neighborhoods, killing forty-eight blacks and burning many buildings. In New Orleans, blacks who were gathering for a meeting were fiercely attacked by a white mob led by the sheriff, who was a former Confederate general. About forty blacks were killed, and many more were wounded.

In February 1866, the Radicals and President Johnson clashed over extending the life of the Freedmen's Bureau. This agency was created during Lincoln's administration to help the newly freed blacks acquire food, clothing, and shelter and to aid them in settling on abandoned lands. It also established schools and hospitals for blacks and assisted them in drawing up fair labor contracts. The president vetoed the bill to continue the Freedmen's Bureau. He argued that it was unconstitutional to permit a federal agency to provide relief functions in peacetime and that the blacks could best advance through their own labor. Johnson's veto was narrowly upheld because the Radical

Republicans failed to muster the two-thirds vote of both houses of Congress needed to override a presidential veto. Not long afterward, however, another Freedmen's Bureau Bill was passed. Although it was vetoed by Johnson, this time the bill's supporters had enough votes to override the president's action.

Many moderates in Congress who had previously agreed with Johnson's lenient policies toward the South were deeply disappointed by his willingness to scuttle the Freedmen's Bureau. They felt the president had given in to white supremacists and showed no genuine concern for the needs of the Southern blacks.

On George Washington's birthday, three days after the president had vetoed the first bill to extend the life of the Freedmen's Bureau, a crowd of Johnson's supporters marched behind a band to the White House to serenade the president and applaud his opposition to the Freedmen's Bureau. Johnson greeted them warmly and then began to read the speech he had prepared. Spurred on by their resounding cheers, the president lost his composure, laid his paper aside, and began ranting wildly about how he hated the Radical Republicans. When he thundered at the audience that there were men in the North as treasonable as any Confederates had been, a voice in the crowd shouted, "Give us their names!"

Fuming with righteous indignation, Johnson replied, "I say Thaddeus Stevens of Pennsylvania, I say Charles Sumner of Massachusetts, I say Wendell Phillips of Massachusetts and others of the same stripe."[11] To suggest that these three prominent Republicans were traitors was clearly beyond the limits of reasonable opinion. This harsh charge revealed that the man in the White House had an uncontrollable temper and appeared to be losing touch with reality.

In April 1866, Congress passed the Civil Rights Bill, designed to provide citizenship and federal protection of their civil rights to the former slaves. Moderates in Congress and nearly all of Johnson's cabinet advised him to sign this bill, but the stubborn president turned down this opportunity to compromise with his opponents. He vetoed the bill, largely on the ground that it violated the rights of the Southern states still not represented in Congress. Johnson's veto was overridden by both houses of Congress; it was now clear that many moderates had deserted the president and accepted the arguments of the Radical Republicans.

The following month Congress proposed the Fourteenth Amendment, which consisted of four parts. The most important part provided the first national definition of citizenship: all persons born or naturalized in the United States (except untaxed Native Americans) were citizens of the United States. The individual states were forbidden to curtail the rights of citizens or to deny them "the equal protection of the laws." The second part said that a state that denied the vote to adult males would have its representation in Congress reduced. The third section disqualified former Confederates from holding national or state offices (but not from voting) unless pardoned by Congress. The fourth section said that the debts of the Union government had to be paid, but the debts acquired by the Confederacy were illegal and thus not to be paid.

The Fourteenth Amendment passed by the required two-thirds vote in both houses of Congress. The president could not veto a constitutional amendment, but Johnson urged the Southern state legislatures not to ratify it. Of the eleven Confederate states, only Tennessee ratified the amendment, and it was quickly readmitted to the Union.

Johnson's opposition to the Fourteenth Amendment spelled his political doom. In the eyes of most Northerners, the president no longer was a staunch Unionist intent on seeking a just and fair solution to reconstruction problems. Instead, he was looked on as a disloyal Southerner, a former slave owner, a despised Democrat serving disgracefully in a Republican administration, and a turncoat who had sold his soul to the white bigots in the South.

The Radical Republicans now were determined to put the whole matter of reconstruction into the hands of Congress and disregard any further interference by the president. In 1867, the Southern states which had followed the reconstruction plan laid down by President Johnson were declared to have no legal status, and the Confederate states were combined into five military districts. An army general was put in charge of each district with orders to rule it as a "conquered province." All adult males, regardless of race, were given the vote. After a state legislature had ratified the Fourteenth Amendment and Congress had approved its constitution, the state could be readmitted to the Union. By the end of 1868, six of the Confederate states were back in the Union, and all were readmitted by mid-1870.

The Radical Republicans' hatred of Johnson grew so intense that they sought ways in Congress to sharply curtail his powers. Congress passed an act depriving the president of command of the army by requiring that he issue all military orders through General Grant. Then the Radicals pushed through Congress the Tenure of Office Act, forbidding the president to remove high-ranking civil officials, including cabinet members, from his administration without the consent of the Senate. This act was intended to protect Secretary of War Edwin Stanton, who vigorously supported the Radicals' reconstruction policies and supervised the army's control of the South.

President Johnson, however, was determined to get rid of Stanton, whom he considered a troublemaker in the cabinet and a spy for the Radicals. He first suspended and later dismissed Stanton from his cabinet without obtaining the consent of the Senate. Thus the president had disobeyed the Tenure of Office Act, and the Radicals moved swiftly to exploit the situation.

The House of Representatives drew up impeachment charges, and Johnson had to stand trial in the Senate. If two-thirds of the Senate found the president guilty of committing "high crimes and misdemeanors," his punishment would be removal from office.

Johnson felt that the Tenure of Office Act was a trap laid by vicious congressional enemies who wanted to get rid of a president they could not control. He believed the act was unconstitutional, since the Constitution imposed no restrictions on the president's dismissing officials in the executive department of the government. So his defense attorneys argued that Johnson had committed no crime by breaking a law that was unconstitutional, and they declared that he should not be forced out of office because his political views were unpopular and different from those held by many members of Congress.

The impeachment vote was exceedingly close. Thirty-five senators voted that Johnson was guilty and nineteen senators (including seven Republicans) voted that he was not guilty. Since two-thirds of the senators must vote against the president to oust him from office, Johnson was spared—by a single vote—the worst indignity that can befall a president.

Although Johnson was both conscientious and courageous in tackling the reconstruction problems he inherited from Lincoln, he obviously was not well qualified for the job he had to perform. Since he refused to consider various alternatives and then forge policies that most Northerners could agree on, he found himself alienated from majority opinion and unable to act effectively. Since he would not compromise, Johnson could not lead.

Had Lincoln lived, no doubt he too would have clashed with Congress. Before his death, he had already locked horns with the legislators over the Wade-Davis Bill, which he vetoed. But, according to the historians Thomas A. Bailey and David M. Kennedy, "The surefooted and experienced Lincoln could hardly have blundered into the same quicksand that engulfed Johnson." Lincoln would have had the enormous advantage of being regarded after the Civil War as a *victorious* president, a public hero who had won the affection and esteem of a grateful people. "Enjoying battle-tested powers of leadership," Bailey and Kennedy said, "he possessed in full measure tact, sweet reasonableness, and an uncommon amount of common sense. Andrew Johnson, hot-tempered and impetuous, lacked all of these priceless qualities."[12]

CHAPTER TWO

JAMES A. GARFIELD

Murdered by a Crazed Office Seeker

On November 19, 1831, James Abram Garfield was born in a log cabin built by his father in Cuyahoga County, Ohio, southeast of the city of Cleveland. Having never known his father, who died when he was two years old, James grew up in poverty. From an early age, he and his brother and two sisters had to work hard on the small family farm. James could leave the farm and attend a nearby school only three months every winter, but his teachers recognized that he was a bright student with much academic promise.

James dreamed of becoming a sailor and visiting exotic ports around the world. At the age of seventeen, he went to Cleveland with the hope that a large shipping company would hire him. But he had to settle for a menial job on a canal boat, and the farthest he sailed was to Pittsburgh. During the six weeks that he worked on the canal boat, he fell overboard fourteen times, a dangerous experience since James could not swim.

His mother urged James to go back to school and study

for a safer occupation. In 1849 he enrolled at an academy in Chester, Ohio. One of his classmates was Lucretia Rudolph, the daughter of a farmer who had helped found the Western Reserve Eclectic Institute (later called Hiram Institute) at Hiram, Ohio. Lucretia and James began a long courtship; they started dating while in their teens but did not marry until 1858, when they were both twenty-six.

In 1851 Garfield began attending the Eclectic Institute, which was somewhat similar to a junior college. An ambitious student, he excelled in nearly all his subjects and was especially talented in debating. He worked his way through school as a janitor and a teacher in an elementary school. By 1854 he had saved enough money for a college education and went to Williams College in Williamstown, Massachusetts, where he was enrolled as a junior. His grades were high, and he did especially well in foreign languages. Garfield mastered German, Greek, and Latin.

When he returned to Ohio in 1856, the youthful scholar began teaching classical languages at the Eclectic Institute, and the following year he was named its principal. But Garfield's interests stretched far beyond the classroom. A deeply religious man, he often preached sermons at the Disciples of Christ Church. He also became interested in law and politics. In his spare time, he studied law and was admitted to the Ohio bar in 1859.

Garfield's first plunge into the political arena occurred in 1859, when he ran successfully for the state senate on the ticket of the new Republican party. The next year he campaigned ardently for Abraham Lincoln in the presidential election. The scholar-turned-politician was becoming a Republican leader in the Ohio state legislature when the Civil War broke out.

Volunteering to serve in the Union army, Garfield was commissioned a lieutenant colonel. This shrewd, well-educated officer demonstrated on the battlefield his ability to lead men, and during the course of the war he was promoted to higher ranks, ultimately to the rank of major general. In January 1862, Garfield's troops defeated a larger Confederate force at Middle Creek in eastern Kentucky. Later he fought in the crucial battles of Shiloh and Chickamauga. In a daring ride at Chickamauga, when his horse was wounded under enemy fire, Garfield managed to convey important information to Union soldiers along the entire front.

While still in uniform, Garfield was elected to the House of Representatives in 1863; a few months later, at the age of thirty-one, he took his seat in Congress. The former canal boat worker impressed his colleagues not only with his intelligence and oratory but also with his tolerance, fairness, and skill at proposing compromises. Garfield also was popular with the voters back home in Ohio, who re-elected him to eight more terms in the House of Representatives. During the administration of President Rutherford B. Hayes (who declined to run for a second term), Garfield was the highest ranking Republican in the House, the party's minority leader. Then, in January 1880, Garfield was elected to the U.S. Senate, for a term beginning in March 1881.

When Senator-elect Garfield arrived in Chicago as a delegate to the Republican national convention in June 1880, he had no intention of running for the presidency. Some of his friends and a few newspaper stories suggested that he would be a good presidential candidate; one friend predicted that if the convention were deadlocked, he might get the nomination. Garfield, however, did not agree. "I should be greatly distressed if I thought otherwise," he wrote in his diary. "There is too much possible work in me to set so near an end to it all, as that would do."[1] Garfield knew that ever since Lincoln's death fifteen years before, Congress, not the executive, had been the most powerful branch of the national government. It seemed likely that the legislative branch would continue its dominant role, and Garfield wanted to stay in Congress.

The newly elected senator had two important reasons

for attending the 1880 Republican convention. First, he had agreed to be the campaign manager for Treasury Secretary John Sherman, a fellow Ohioan who was seeking the presidential nomination. Second, Garfield wanted to do all in his power to help prevent the nomination of Ulysses S. Grant for a third term in the White House. Grant's first two terms, which had ended in 1877, had been riddled with scandals, and the president had been dominated by unsavory aides and unscrupulous party bosses, who pursued various forms of graft and corruption. After the former general retired from the presidency, he embarked on a world tour that lasted more than two years and gave him the opportunity to be wined and dined by Queen Victoria, rulers of other countries, and countless celebrities. With much fanfare, Grant returned to the United States an international hero, and he was persuaded by his old political cronies to run again for the presidency.

At that time the Republican party was split into two warring factions. The Stalwarts, who had supported Grant in his two previous elections and backed him again in 1880, were the more conservative faction. Their opponents, called the Half-Breeds, claimed they were more moderate than the Stalwarts. The Half-Breeds' candidate for the presidency in 1880 was James G. Blaine, the popular senator from Maine.

Garfield listened as Senator Roscoe Conkling, an influential Stalwart and the powerful boss of the Republican political machine in New York, delivered an emotional seconding speech for Grant's nomination. Suave, handsome, and exceedingly arrogant, Conkling lashed out at the Half-Breeds, calling them "charlatans" and "tramps." A short time later, Garfield addressed the convention. He nominated Sherman and described the secretary of the Treasury as a candidate of neither faction who could create party harmony and help bridge the gulf between the Stalwarts and the Half-Breeds.

The results of the first convention ballot were Grant

304 votes, Blaine 284, Sherman 93, and 74 scattered among three other candidates. For ballot after ballot, the voting stayed about the same. On the thirty-third ballot, Grant had 309 votes, Blaine 276, Sherman 110, and Garfield 1. Never before in its history had the Republican party been so completely stalemated in its selection of a presidential candidate.

Finally, some of Garfield's supporters decided to break the deadlock, even though they had not received his consent. On the thirty-fourth ballot, the Wisconsin delegation cast sixteen votes for Garfield. Immediately, the Ohio congressman sprang to his feet and declared, "No man has a right, without the consent of the person voted for, to announce that person's name and vote for him in this convention. Such consent I have not given."[2]

Despite Garfield's protest, the weary delegates responded enthusiastically to Wisconsin's signal to nominate a compromise candidate. Supporters of Blaine and Sherman began flocking to the Garfield banner. He won the nomination on the thirty-sixth ballot, with 399 votes to 306 for Grant. Only the Stalwart delegates remained stubbornly committed to the former president, who had been their original choice.

The Republican leaders knew they could not elect Garfield without Stalwart support. So to appease that wing of the party, the convention nominated for vice president the Stalwart Chester A. Arthur, one of Conkling's closest associates in his New York political machine. In fact, Arthur had been so deeply involved in questionable partisan activities while serving as customs collector at the port of New York that President Hayes had removed him from office.

John Sherman heartily approved the presidential nomination of his former campaign manager because he considered Garfield a capable, experienced, honest man. But Sherman was disgusted that the convention had named Arthur as Garfield's running mate. He angrily asserted that

Arthur's nomination was a "ridiculous burlesque . . . inspired by a desire to defeat the ticket."[3]

Roscoe Conkling, however, was not placated by the party's decision to run Arthur for the vice presidency. He even tried unsuccessfully to convince Arthur that he should refuse the nomination, partly because the office of vice president seemed so unimportant and partly because he felt that the Republicans would lose the White House to the Democrats in the fall. Conkling intimated that most Stalwarts would play no active part in the presidential campaign.

Without the help of the Stalwarts, Garfield knew that he could not defeat the Democratic presidential nominee, General Winfield Hancock, a Civil War hero. During the campaign, he met privately in New York with Stalwart chieftains, who wanted him to promise that Senator Conkling could have the final say in appointing New Yorkers to political jobs.

Accounts of this meeting varied, but apparently Garfield promised no more than that he would consult with Conkling and other New York Republican leaders about federal offices to be filled in that state. In his diary he wrote that he had emerged from the conference with "no trades— no shackles."[4]

Toward the end of the campaign, Conkling quit pouting long enough to deliver some speeches for the Republican ticket in New York, Indiana, and Ohio. Garfield probably would have won his home state anyway, but without New York and Indiana, which he carried by very slim margins, he would have lost the election. Hancock was victorious in all the former states of the Confederacy (known as the Democrats' "Solid South"), plus eight other states.

Garfield won the electoral vote 214 to 155. But the popular vote was the closest in the history of presidential races: Garfield's margin of victory was only 1,898 votes out of a total of more than 9 million votes cast.[5]

The new president had long been a champion of civil

service reform. When he was a congressman, he had warned his colleagues that the pressure they exerted on federal agencies to hire the job applicants that they sponsored was a major cause of inefficient government. Garfield declared:

> ━━━━━━━ *We crowd the doors; we fill the corridors; Senators and Representatives throng the offices and Bureaus until the public business is obstructed, the patience of officers is worn out, and sometimes for fear of losing their places by our influence, they at last give way and appoint men, not because they are fit for the positions but because we ask it.* [6]

In his inaugural address as president, Garfield stated emphatically that civil service could never operate on a satisfactory basis until it was regulated by law. But Congress was reluctant to pass such a law, chiefly because senators and representatives had long enjoyed the privilege of rewarding their faithful and generous supporters with government jobs.

Shortly after Garfield moved into the White House, he clashed openly with the two Stalwart senators from New York, Conkling and Thomas C. Platt. He appointed a hated enemy of the Stalwarts, William H. Robertson, to serve as the customs collector of the port of New York. No appointment that the president could have made would have been so hard a blow to Conkling and Platt as this. The two New York Stalwarts furiously denounced Robertson on the Senate floor, but they failed to convince a majority of their colleagues that his nomination should be immediately rejected. Instead, the senators postponed voting on the Robertson appointment. Then, dramatizing their ultimate protest, Conkling and Platt resigned their seats in the Senate. (At that time state legislatures elected U.S. senators, and Conkling and Platt felt certain that the New York State legislature would reelect them.)

Other Stalwart senators suggested to the president that this issue could be easily resolved if he would simply withdraw Robertson's nomination. But Garfield was resolved to assert his authority as president by supporting his nomination until the Senate acted on it. "I wanted it known soon," he told a friend, "whether I was the registering Clerk of the Senate or the Executive of the government."[7]

The Senate finally confirmed Robertson's appointment. Soon afterward, Conkling and Platt discovered that they could not take the New York State legislature for granted: it did not reelect them to the Senate. Conkling felt so humiliated that he retired from politics; Platt needed many years of patient effort to become a powerful figure in the New York Republican party again.

When he became president, Garfield was constantly besieged by hundreds and hundreds of eager job seekers, who made it difficult for him to find time for his other work. But numerous government positions had to be filled, sometimes as many as fifty a day. Since Garfield personally knew only a small fraction of the applicants, he had to rely either on his own intuition or on the advice of others in deciding which prospects probably would be efficient and honest. More than ever before, Garfield was determined to call for civil service reform.

"I feel like crying out in the agony of my soul against the greed for office and its consumption of my time," he lamented. "My services ought to be worth more to the government than to be spent thus." At another time, he observed, "My day is frittered away by the personal seeking of people, when it ought to be given to the great problems which concern the whole country. Some civil service reform will come by necessity after the wearisome years of wasted presidents have paved the way for it."[8]

One of the most persistent job seekers was Charles J. Guiteau, a mentally deranged thirty-nine-year-old man, who had met failure in the three types of work he had attempted—journalism, law, and leading a religious crusade. In his crazed mind, he thought that because he had supported the Republican party in the 1880 election he should be rewarded with a consulship, either in Paris or in Vienna. Guiteau stalked the corridors of the White House and State Department, pleading his case to anyone who would listen. He sent numerous letters to the president and Secretary of State James G. Blaine, claiming that he was qualified for a position in the foreign service.

On May 13, 1881, Guiteau once again approached Blaine; this time he demanded the diplomatic post at Paris. His patience at the breaking point, Blaine roared at Guiteau, "Never bother me again about the Paris consulship as long as you live!"[9] That same day, Conkling and Platt resigned from the Senate; the newspapers reported the action as a great defeat for the Stalwarts.

Guiteau considered himself a loyal Stalwart, and, linking the resignations of Conkling and Platt with his own failure to obtain a government job, he decided that President Garfield was trying to crush the Stalwarts. As a result, Guiteau became convinced that God had ordered him to murder the president. He wrote on June 20, "The President's removal is an act of God. I am clear in my purpose to remove the President. . . . It will unite the Republican party and save the Republic. . . ."[10]

With this in mind, Guiteau purchased a relatively expensive silver-mounted English pistol. (He wanted a handsome pistol because he felt certain it would be displayed in a museum after the assassination.) After stalking the president for a few weeks and bypassing at least two opportunities to shoot him, he rose early on July 2 and began preparations to kill Garfield at the Baltimore and Potomac railroad station. He had learned that the president was scheduled to leave that morning by train on a vacation trip.

Garfield and Blaine were walking through the depot waiting room when suddenly a loud shot was heard a few feet behind them, quickly followed by another. The president sank to the floor. The first bullet had grazed his right arm, but the other had entered his body to the right of his spinal cord.

Guiteau was caught by a police officer, and after he was hauled outside the depot, he called out, "I did it and will go to jail for it. Arthur is President and I am a Stalwart."[11] (At his trial, Guiteau pleaded not guilty by reason of insanity, but the jury found him guilty, and he was hanged on June 30, 1882.)

The stricken president lingered between life and death for more than ten weeks. Doctors repeatedly probed his back wound with bare fingers and unsterilized instruments, a common practice of that period, in order to find the bullet, but they were unable to locate it. Alexander Graham Bell was summoned to bring to the president's bedside a device he had invented for locating metal, which was a forerunner of the modern land-mine detector. When Bell applied the metal detector to Garfield's body, only a static blur appeared on the screen. (Later it was believed that the metal coils on Garfield's bed mattress caused the detector to malfunction.)

Blood poisoning set in, and the suffocating heat in the nation's capital made the weakening president very uncomfortable. He asked to be moved by train to a seaside cottage on the shore at Elberon, New Jersey. All through one night, more than five thousand men labored to lay about a half mile of track from the Pennsylvania Railroad's line to the Elberon cottage. After Garfield arrived at the cottage, he seemed at first to rally in the cooler weather, but bronchopneumonia developed and he died on September 19, 1881.

Even before Garfield's death, a frightening concern about his successor gripped the country. Chester Arthur had woefully little experience in high-level government service. Before becoming vice president, he had never been elected to any political office and had been fired from the only public job he had ever held—at the New York customhouse. His only previous claim to fame was serving in Conkling's political machine. He never would have been nominated for the vice presidency except to appease the Stalwarts, who were furious when Grant was denied a possible third term in the White House.

Prominent Republican leaders were mortified by the thought of what might happen to the country with Arthur in the White House. Former President Hayes confided to his diary: "The death of the President at this time would be a national calamity whose consequences we can not now confidently conjecture. Arthur for President! Conkling the power behind the throne, superior to the throne! . . ." Senator Sherman wrote to Hayes that he had "strong anticipations of the evil to come" from an Arthur administration. [12]

President Arthur, however, surprised even his sternest critics. Though little good was expected of him, he became an example of the politician who grows in office. Undoubtedly his foremost goal as president was to leave a record of honesty and efficiency that would far overshadow the questionable practices of earlier years when he had been accused of handing out government jobs to friends and soliciting donations from those employed by his political machine.

The new president attempted to steer a middle course between the opposing factions of the Republican party. Although he gave appointments to some Stalwarts and urged the election of others, he exercised caution by supporting men of integrity and ability. He retained Robertson, the Stalwarts' hated enemy, as the New York collector of customs. When scandals in the Post Office Department were publicized, Arthur ordered his attorney general to prosecute "with the utmost vigor of the law," even though two of the chief culprits had been friends of his.

Garfield's assassination by a frustrated office seeker wakened the nation to the need for radical changes in the civil service system. Arthur called for such changes in his first annual message to Congress. But the legislators ignored his request, as they had those of former Presidents Hayes and Garfield when they had asked for civil service reform. However, neither a doggedly determined president nor an outraged public would let this issue die. In his second annual message to Congress, Arthur again emphatically demanded civil service reform.

Finally, in January 1883, Congress passed a Civil Service Bill that had been introduced by Ohio's Democratic senator, George Pendleton. It provided that 10 percent of all federal jobs were to be placed under the merit system, with future appointments to those government jobs determined by open competitive examinations. The president had the authority to expand the number of jobs requiring civil service examinations. Soon many of the civilian positions in the federal government were governed by civil service regulations. One of the most unfair practices of the old spoils system—assessing the salaries of government employees for political purposes—was prohibited. A bipartisan Civil Service Commission, appointed by the president, was set up to oversee the operation of the new system.

President Arthur eagerly signed Pendleton's bill into law. Then he carefully selected well-qualified persons from both major political parties to sit on the first Civil Service Commission. The Pendleton Act became the crowning achievement of Arthur's administration. Ironically, Arthur—the former spoilsman—was the president who ushered in the reforms that made the first significant dents in political machines that dated back at least to the time of Andrew Jackson.

In other ways Arthur was a forceful president. Recognizing that American naval power was inadequate, he pushed through Congress appropriations for new steel ships and earned the title "father of the United States's modern navy." He spoke out in favor of regulating interstate commerce, and two years after he left the presidency, Congress passed the Interstate Commerce Act. Arthur courageously vetoed "pork barrel" legislation that he felt would spend taxpayers' money on unnecessary projects involving rivers and harbors, but Congress overrode his vetoes. He also clashed with the lawmakers when they tried to exclude Chinese laborers for twenty years and forced Congress to reduce the exclusion of Chinese immigrants to a period of ten years.

When Arthur left the White House after a single term in office, his presidency was praised much more widely than it was condemned. The author Mark Twain observed: "I am but one in 55,000,000; still, in the opinion of this one-fifty-five-millionth of the country's population, it would be hard to better President Arthur's Administration. But don't decide till you hear from the rest."[13]

WILLIAM McKINLEY

Sweeping Changes
Follow His
Death

"McKinley was more than popular—he was beloved," wrote the historian Margaret Leech. "Scores of his associates were his friends, and many of them held him in worshipful admiration. Even his political opponents were attracted by the peculiar sweetness of his personality."[1]

A congenial, kindly man, William McKinley radiated warmth to friends and strangers alike. He enjoyed being with people, sharing their ideas, listening to their problems, laughing at their jokes. Although dignified and statesmanlike in his bearing, he was not haughty or arrogant. Even after he became president, he remained a modest man with simple tastes, and he was genuinely thoughtful to those who surrounded him.

Like Presidents Hayes and Garfield before him, McKinley had his political roots in Ohio. He was born January 29, 1843, in Niles, Ohio, the seventh of nine children. His father was a businessman who had to support his large family on a modest income. William attended the local public school and enjoyed his studies. He was a bright, diligent, religious boy, and his mother hoped he would become a Methodist minister.

At seventeen William entered Allegheny College at Meadville, Pennsylvania, as a junior, but he had to drop out of school after one term because of illness. By the time he recuperated, the family finances were depleted, and he had to go to work instead of returning to college. Until the Civil War started, he taught school and clerked in a post office.

William served in the Twenty-third Ohio Volunteer Infantry from June 1861, when he was eighteen, to July 1865. During these years in the Union army, William moved up in rank from a private to a major. He saw action in some of the bloodiest battles in the war, and his commanding officer, Col. Rutherford B. Hayes, commended young McKinley for outstanding service and exceptional bravery.

After the war, McKinley studied law, was admitted to the Ohio bar, and set up practice in Canton, Ohio. There he met Ida Saxton, the daughter of a prominent banker. They fell in love and were married in 1871. The McKinleys had two daughters, but one died in infancy and the other at the age of four. After the first child died, Mrs. McKinley began having convulsions, accompanied by loss of consciousness. She remained an epileptic the rest of her life, suffered frequent seizures, and became completely dependent on her husband.

McKinley believed in the principles of the Republican party and was active in political affairs in his community. In 1876 he was elected to the House of Representatives, and he served in Congress for twelve of the next fourteen years. Then, in 1891, Ohio voters selected him as their governor and reelected him two years later. In the congressional campaign of 1894, McKinley delivered speeches throughout the nation in behalf of Republican candidates. At that time the country was in the midst of an economic depression that had struck during the presidential administration of the Democrat Grover Cleveland. In his speeches McKinley blamed the Democrats for the depression and predicted that conditions would improve under Republican leadership. The Ohio governor's speeches had such an optimistic tone that he came to be known as "the advance agent of prosperity." During this congressional campaign, McKinley was carefully laying the groundwork for his own run for the presidency two years later.

With the financial support and shrewd guidance of Marcus A. Hanna, an Ohio industrialist and politician, McKinley easily won the Republican nomination for president in 1896. The vice presidential nominee was Garret Hobart of New Jersey, who had held various offices within his state government.

McKinley's Democratic opponent was the former Nebraska congressman William Jennings Bryan, a spellbinding speaker who frequently brought cheering audiences to their feet. Bryan vigorously supported bimetallism, a money system based on both gold and silver that would permit the unlimited coinage of silver. McKinley and many Republicans staunchly opposed bimetallism; they insisted that basing money in circulation on silver in addition to gold would lead to runaway inflation and economic peril.

Bryan launched a hectic campaign, crisscrossing the nation as he fervently sought to convince the voters that the unlimited coinage of silver would cure the country's financial ills. According to his own estimates, he covered more than eighteen thousand miles and made about six hundred speeches to possibly 5 million people.[2]

McKinley, on the other hand, let the voters come to him. He stayed at home in Canton, Ohio, addressing groups and answering questions from his front porch. People came by the thousands in specially chartered trains to see and hear the Republican nominee. Most of them went back home feeling certain that McKinley was a safe and sound candidate—someone they could trust not to "rock the boat" by proposing radical changes, such as Bryan's bimetallism.

McKinley defeated Bryan by a margin of 271 electoral

votes to 176. The popular vote was closer; the Republican candidate won by about 500 thousand votes out of nearly 14 million cast. McKinley captured the Northeast and most of the Midwest, while Bryan carried every southern state and all the western states except California and Oregon.

In many ways McKinley was the perfect model of the business community's president. He advocated high tariffs to protect American industries from cheaper goods produced in other countries. He believed in a money system based only on the gold standard (which he called "sound money"). He opposed high taxes, government regulation of business, and large federal expenditures.

McKinley also believed that in the last decade of the nineteenth century the United States should emerge as a major actor on the world stage. He led the nation into the Spanish-American War, which freed Cuba and permitted the United States to acquire the Philippines, Puerto Rico, and Guam. Under McKinley, the United States also annexed Hawaii (1898) and Wake Island and divided the Samoan islands with Germany (1899). McKinley's Department of State established the "open-door" policy in China, which allowed the United States to obtain an economic foothold in that part of Asia.

Although McKinley was a strong friend to business interests and a prominent world leader, during his presidency he virtually ignored some of the nation's most urgent problems. The companies and corporations which, after the Civil War, had grown by leaps and bounds into huge trusts and monopolies, ran roughshod over smaller industries, farmers, and consumers. Unregulated railroads were benefiting large shippers at the expense of small ones, and unions had difficulty gaining a better standard of living for workers. The country's natural resources, once so rich and plentiful, were being depleted rapidly. And the public had no way of knowing whether the food and medicine purchased at local stores were safe to consume.

Even though these serious problems were largely side-stepped by McKinley, the president continued to be well liked by millions of Americans, and there was no Republican opposition to his bid for a second term in the White House. But Vice President Hobart had died about six months before the Republican national convention assembled in June 1900, so the race for the vice presidential nomination was wide open. McKinley did not have a preference for a running mate, and he asked Mark Hanna, his campaign manager, not to influence the delegates. Hanna agreed to let the delegates select whomever they wished as the vice presidential nominee, but he later regretted this decision.

One Republican leader who did have a vice presidential candidate in mind was Thomas C. Platt. (After the New York State legislature had refused to reelect Platt to the Senate in 1881, he worked his way back up the political ladder until he again became both a New York party boss and a U.S. senator.) Platt's choice for the 1900 vice presidential nomination was Governor Theodore Roosevelt of New York. He wanted Roosevelt to be selected not because he liked and respected him; quite the opposite, Roosevelt had pushed through the state legislature a series of reforms that Platt had strongly opposed. Now Platt wanted to get rid of the troublesome governor by helping to put him in the office of vice president, where he could no longer meddle in New York's political affairs.

When Hanna learned about Platt's scheme, he was furious. He knew about Roosevelt's reputation as a reformer, and Hanna—himself a political boss—did not want such an uncontrollable activist on the national ticket. "Don't any of you realize," he protested to the other party chieftains, "that there's only one life between that madman and the Presidency?"[3]

Roosevelt, who was often referred to as "T.R.," was popular with the convention delegates, and the forty-one-year-old governor clinched the vice presidential nomination before the balloting began. Then he undertook a strenuous election campaign, speaking throughout the country and winning support from large throngs of voters.

William Jennings Bryan was again the Democratic contender for the presidency, pitted in a rematch against McKinley. The economic depression had subsided during McKinley's first term, and the public gave him a strong vote of confidence. The McKinley-Roosevelt ticket in 1900 won more electoral votes and more popular votes than the McKinley-Hobart ticket had achieved in 1896.

Roosevelt was bored and restless in the office of vice president; his only official duties were to preside over the Senate and cast a tie-breaking vote in those rare instances when a measure before the Senate had the same number of votes for and against it. The new vice president had boundless energy, and he was accustomed to holding jobs that called for vigorous activity and usually attracted newspaper headlines. In previous positions—as a member of the New York State legislature, a civil service commissioner, a New York City police commissioner, assistant secretary of the Navy, a lieutenant colonel in the Spanish-American War "Rough Riders" cavalry regiment, and governor of New York—he had plunged himself into his work with enormous enthusiasm and unflagging dedication. Now, as vice president, he felt he was frittering away his time doing nothing important and attracting no public attention.

An event that occurred on September 6, 1901, dramatically changed Roosevelt's situation and significantly altered the course of American history. On that date President McKinley was shot by Leon Czolgosz, a twenty-eight-year-old unemployed mill worker. Czolgosz had fanatical political beliefs and called himself an anarchist (a person who wants all governments destroyed and a world without rulers or laws).

McKinley had attended the Pan-American Exposition in Buffalo, New York. On the afternoon of the fateful day, the president was holding a public reception in the ornate

Temple of Music. A large number of people had lined up to shake his hand and wish him well. In that line was Czolgosz, whose right hand held a pistol concealed beneath a white cloth that looked like a bandage.

As Czolgosz approached McKinley, he extended his left hand as if to greet him. Then suddenly he fired two shots at the president's abdomen. One bullet struck a button on McKinley's vest and did not pierce the skin. The other penetrated the stomach and may have lodged in the pancreas. Startled and dazed, McKinley staggered backward and fell into the arms of a guard. As other officers swarmed over Czolgosz, the president mumbled, "Be easy with him, boys."[4]

McKinley was rushed to a hospital, where an operation was performed. Doctors hunted in vain for the bullet, cleaned the abdominal cavity as best they could, and sewed shut the surface wound. The president seemed to improve. His temperature began falling, and he was taken to a friend's home in Buffalo to recuperate. On September 12, however, his condition worsened, and two days later he died. The cause of death was apparently gangrene poisoning. Even after a four-hour search during the autopsy, the fatal bullet was never located.

Immediately after the shooting, Czolgosz told the authorities that he had carried out his "duty" to strike down a president who he felt was indifferent and hostile to the "working people." "I didn't believe," he said, "[that] one man should have so much and another should have none."[5]

Czolgosz's trial lasted only about nine hours, and the jury found him guilty of murder. Before being put to death in the electric chair, he showed no remorse for the horrible crime he had committed. His last words were, "I killed the president because he was the enemy of the people—the good working people. I am not sorry for my crime."[6]

The vice president whom Mark Hanna had called a madman suddenly was elevated to the presidency. At forty-two years of age, Theodore Roosevelt became the nation's youngest chief executive. Energetic, dynamic, aggressive, he brought about major economic and social changes that McKinley never sought while he was in the White House.

Roosevelt called his domestic program the Square Deal. He said it was based on the country's need for (1) regulation (but not the destruction) of big business, (2) broader control of the railroads, (3) conservation of natural resources, and (4) a concerted attack on the serious social problems that affected large numbers of Americans.

The new president believed in capitalism, but he wanted to protect it against unfair practices that he felt could lead to its destruction. He was deeply concerned about the illegal combinations of companies that had been established in the last third of the nineteenth century to stifle competition and control prices and rates. To restore competition—the cornerstone of free enterprise—illegal trusts and monopolies had to be dissolved.

Since Congress refused to give the president new anti-trust legislation, Roosevelt used the nearly dormant Sherman Antitrust Act of 1890 to battle the monopolies. First, he ordered his attorney general to file a lawsuit against the huge Northern Securities Company, a holding company organized to monopolize transportation in the Northwest by merging three railroad lines. The case was decided by the Supreme Court, with the justices voting five to four that the Northern Securities Company had violated the Sherman Antitrust Act and must be broken up. Later, the Roosevelt administration brought antitrust suits against two dozen other large business combinations, including those in the oil, steel, beef, and tobacco industries. These actions earned Roosevelt the nickname of "trust buster," and they were generally approved by an appreciative public that regarded the president as the defender of the people against the tyranny of predatory commercial interests.

In 1902, Roosevelt faced a major challenge to his presidential leadership when the United Mine Workers called a strike of 150,000 coal miners for higher wages and better working conditions. At that time, conditions in the coal fields were among the most miserable in the country, and the workers seemed entitled to their demands. But the operators of the mines refused to bargain or even consult with the union representatives.

The strike, which had begun in May, still was not settled by October, when the first cool weather arrived in much of the country. Fearful that millions of Americans would be without heat in their homes and places of business, President Roosevelt urged both sides to have the strike arbitrated (settled by a neutral referee). The workers agreed to his proposal, but the owners again said they would make no settlement except on their terms.

Acting in what he considered the public interest, the president threatened to send federal troops to seize and operate the mines. This blunt warning forced the owners to agree that they would accept the results of an impartial commission's investigation of the dispute. The commission awarded the miners a 10 percent wage increase and ordered the improvement of working conditions.

For the first time in the history of the United States, a president had used his power to bring both sides together to end a strike. When critics accused Roosevelt of being prolabor, he replied, "My business is to see fair play among all men, capitalists or wageworkers" and to face national crises with "immediate and vigorous executive action." All he wanted, the president said, was "to see to it that every man has a square deal, no more and no less."[7]

One of the railroads' worst abuses was the common practice of giving lower rates to large shippers; most farmers and other small shippers were infuriated because they had to pay higher rates. So, in 1903, Roosevelt convinced Congress to pass the Elkins Act, which made it illegal for railroads to charge rates that were different from those in their published rate schedules. In the same year, Congress expanded the federal government by adding a Department of Commerce and Labor. It had the power to investigate and report on the operation of corporations engaged in interstate commerce (business involving more than one state).

Roosevelt showed much more interest in the profitable development of unused lands than had McKinley. He pushed through Congress in 1902 the Newlands Reclamation Act, which set aside almost all the money collected from the sale of public lands in sixteen western and southwestern states to finance construction and maintenance of irrigation projects in arid states.

Roosevelt ran in 1904 for a second term in the White House. His Democratic opponent was the little-known Alton B. Parker, a New York Appeals Court judge. T.R., riding a crest of mounting popularity, defeated Parker easily, sweeping every section of the country except the South, which had voted solidly Democratic since the end of Reconstruction.

Beginning his second term, Roosevelt considered stricter railroad regulation a major legislative objective, but he faced months of stiff opposition from congressional conservatives. Finally, in June 1906, Congress passed the Hepburn Act, which greatly strengthened the Interstate Commerce Commission. It gave that body the authority to fix fair and reasonable railroad rates. The Hepburn Act also extended the commission's jurisdiction to include express and sleeping-car trains, oil pipelines, ferries, terminals, and bridges. The act restricted sharply the granting of free passes and prohibited railroads from carrying commodities produced by companies in which they held an interest.

Two measures passed during Roosevelt's administration with the president's wholehearted approval provided important health benefits for the public. Prompted by Upton Sinclair's *The Jungle*, a book exposing unsanitary conditions in the meat-packing industry, Congress passed the Meat Inspection Act (June 1906). It required the enforcement of sanitary regulations at packing plants and government inspection of meat sold in interstate commerce. A companion measure, the Pure Food and Drug Act, forbade the manufacture, sale, or transportation of fraudulently labeled foods and drugs sold in interstate commerce. It also prohibited food and drug companies from adding inferior or impure materials to their products.

The West always held great interest for Roosevelt. There he had enjoyed the rigors of outdoor life, and there he had often hunted big game. The conservation of its vast forests and wildlife was one of his chief concerns. Acting under the Forest Reserve Act of 1891, he set aside more than 148 million acres of timberland as national forest areas. He had as many national parks created as all the previous presidents combined had established. T.R. also set up fifty-one wildlife refuges and sixteen national monuments. He worked to preserve the scenic beauty of the Grand Canyon, the Petrified Forest, Niagara Falls, and other spectacular natural areas that he believed were the heritage of all present and future Americans.

Before Roosevelt left the presidency, he had more than 80 million acres of mineral lands withdrawn from public sale. Another 1.5 million acres of waterpower sites were set aside. In 1908, the president underscored the need for cooperative action to preserve the nation's natural resources by convening a White House Conservation Conference. Attended by the governors of thirty-four states, congressional leaders, cabinet members, and Supreme Court justices, the conference succeeded in bringing conservation problems to widespread public attention.

In foreign affairs, Roosevelt put into practice what came to be called "big stick diplomacy" (based on his often-quoted statement, "Speak softly and carry a big stick"). He helped engineer the revolt of Panama against Colombia and then moved quickly to lease land from the new Panamanian government for a canal that linked the Atlantic and Pacific oceans. Canal construction began during Roosevelt's administration, and, although it was not completed until five years after he left the White House, T.R. considered his role in helping to provide a remarkable interoceanic canal one of his proudest accomplishments.

Claiming he was upholding the Monroe Doctrine, Roosevelt intervened in the affairs of the Dominican Republic when it was threatened by European creditors. He ordered U.S. agents to collect Dominican customs (import taxes) and divide the receipts between the Dominican government and the countries to which it owed money. Again basing his policy on the Monroe Doctrine, T.R. proudly declared that he had put pressure on Germany to arbitrate its claims against Venezuela for unpaid debts. To dramatize American might, the president sent the Great White Fleet of sixteen battleships on a cruise around the world, defying those critics who feared that this highly publicized show of strength might antagonize other nations. For these sweeping actions in the realm of foreign affairs, Roosevelt was praised by many Americans as a forceful president who had rightfully asserted the power and authority of the United States at a time when it was moving boldly into the twentieth century. Other Americans sharply rebuked the youthful chief executive, saying that he often behaved in a dangerously belligerent manner and pursued saber-rattling policies that helped spread the belief that the United States bullied its weaker neighbors in the Western Hemisphere.

Aggressive by nature, arrogant at times, and always eager to bask in the limelight, Roosevelt was much different from his predecessor, the mild-mannered, modest McKinley. Twice the voters had elected McKinley to the highest office in the land largely because he could be counted on to make few ripples on the placid political scene. After McKinley's assassination brought Roosevelt into the White House, the former "Rough Rider" churned the waves of change, starting new domestic and foreign policies, demanding new legislation, and providing long overdue reforms that improved the lives of millions of people.

CHAPTER FOUR

HUEY LONG

A
Strident Voice
Is Silenced

For many decades Winn Parish (county) in north central Louisiana was a breeding place for radical ideas. One of the most impoverished areas in the South, it was a land of rough red clay and thin, poor soil, where farmers had to struggle hard to eke out a scant living. The toiling farmers of Winn resented the relative prosperity enjoyed by large plantation owners in more productive parts of the state, and when the Civil War broke out, they felt that the Confederacy would benefit only the rich landholders. So, in early 1861, they instructed their delegate to the state's secession convention to vote against the secession of Louisiana from the Union. After Louisiana joined the Confederacy, many Winn farmers refused to take up arms against the North, and seventy-three of them even sent a petition to Gen. Ulysses S. Grant, pledging their loyalty to the Union.

Socialism never attracted a large number of followers in the United States, but in the early years of the twentieth century this radical movement appealed to many poverty-stricken farm families in Winn. More than one-third of Winn voters cast their ballots in 1912 for the socialist presidential candidate, Eugene V. Debs, and the town of Winnfield elected Socialist candidates to all the municipal offices.

One of the most powerful, outspoken radicals in American history, Huey Pierce Long, Jr., was born near Winnfield in 1893. Huey P. Long, Sr., was one of Winnfield's largest landowners and more prosperous citizens by the time his nine children were born. But he had experienced poverty in his youth, and in 1935 (after his son Huey had become a senator) he said to a reporter, "There wants to be a revolution, I tell you. I seen this domination of capital, seen it for seventy years. What do these rich folks care for the poor man?" Then he concluded, "Maybe you're surprised to hear me talk like that. Well, it was just such talk that my boy was raised under."[1]

Young Huey was a bright student, read widely, and became a champion debater in high school. When he was not at school, he sometimes worked in his father's cotton fields, but he hated this monotonous physical labor and vowed never to become a farmer. At thirteen he took a part-time job in the print shop of the Winnfield newspaper, and a few years later he left school to become a traveling salesman. Visiting one southern town after another, he sold furniture, soap, patent medicines, and Cottolene, a cottonseed-oil substitute for cooking lard.

Already a flamboyant showman with a persuasive sales pitch, Huey would stage pie-baking contests in which the bakers used his Cottolene product. One of these contests in Shreveport, Louisiana, was won by a pretty young woman named Rose McConnell. Huey fell in love with Rose, and they were married in 1913.

About this time, Huey decided to become a lawyer. He first had to go back to high school to get his degree. Then, while continuing as a salesman, he attended the University of Oklahoma. After only a year of undergraduate classes, he felt ready to start law school. Borrowing some money from a brother and a friend, he enrolled at Tulane University Law School, studied sixteen hours a day, and passed every course. He finished the course work, which normally took three years, in one year. Huey then petitioned a court in New Orleans for a special bar examination, and, passing it, he received his license to practice law.

In May 1915, at the age of twenty-one, he moved with Rose back to Winnfield and rented a tiny second-floor room in a bank building for his law office. The only furniture in the office were two kitchen chairs, a cheap table, and a kerosene lamp. Unable to afford a telephone, he persuaded the owner of a shoe store next door to take his calls.

At first Huey had so few clients that he could not pay his bills without working part-time again as a traveling salesman. Slowly, however, his legal practice increased, and he won many workmen's compensation cases in which laborers and their families obtained payments from employers for work-related injuries. Young Huey Long was becoming widely known as a lawyer who championed the cause of poor, underprivileged people, but after a few years he tired of the courtroom and sought a political job in which he could expand his talents and help impoverished people in a larger arena.

In 1918, Long was elected a member of the state Railroad Commission (or Public Service Commission, as it was soon renamed). This powerful state commission regulated the rules and rates not only of railroads, but of telephone and telegraph companies, pipelines, and other utilities. It was a perfect sounding board for Long's campaign to help the ordinary people in their struggle against the big-moneyed interests. For nine years, Commissioner Long fought savagely against the large corporations and utility companies. He constantly pressured railroads to reduce rates, improve services, and extend their lines to rural areas, and he demanded that the huge Standard Oil Company make its pipelines available to small independent oil producers. Long made himself a hero to many voters when he forced cancellation of a telephone rate increase.

Long craved more power than he had as a commissioner, and in 1924, when he was barely thirty-one years old, he ran in the Democratic primary election for governor. Political observers believed he had no chance of winning and predicted he would receive only a few thousand votes. But the young candidate from the red-clay fields of Winn Parish surprised the experts. He carried more parishes than either of his two opponents, and his seventy-four thousand votes was only about ten thousand less than the number recorded for the winner. Long ran especially strong in the poor rural areas of northern Louisiana, and he claimed that he would have won if there had not been a heavy rainstorm on election day that kept many folks away from the polls.

Four years later, in 1928, Long again entered the race for the Democratic nomination for governor. His followers paraded under banners reading, "EVERY MAN A KING, BUT NO ONE WEARS A CROWN." He campaigned feverishly around the state, speaking in school auditoriums and at rural crossroads, courthouse squares, church picnics, and town bandstands. Long made as many as eight speeches in eight different towns and villages in a single day. Sweat poured from his beet-red face and stained his seersucker suit; his voice grew raucous and raspy; his fists repeatedly struck out as if he were flailing an unseen enemy. Always the message was the same: Louisiana was ruled by plutocrats (rich people) who must be stripped of their power, and the other candidates for governor were the puppets of the plutocrats. From the large crowds of farmers and other blue-collar workers came applause, cheers, and the repeated refrain, "Pour it on 'em, Huey."

Long won the Democratic nomination for governor, and the Republican party, which was then very small in Louisiana, put up no candidate for the general election. So the battler from Winn had slashed his way upward to the highest political office in the state, and he had accomplished this feat at the age of thirty-five.

Long had been governor only a short time when it became evident that he intended to rule Louisiana as if it were his personal domain. He used patronage—the power of appointment to government offices—to put his loyal followers into political jobs. One by one, all of the state's administrative commissions and boards came under his complete control. Huey Long became probably the most powerful political boss in American history, and he delighted in his role as a tightfisted dictator. When a political opponent complained to him that he, Long, often violated the state constitution, he arrogantly replied, "I'm the constitution around here now."[2]

Long considered himself a twentieth-century Robin Hood dedicated to the principle of helping the poor people, and this accounted for his enormous popularity with Louisiana's Depression-ridden population. While he was governor, free textbooks were distributed for the first time to every schoolchild in the state. Night schools, where 200,000 illiterates were taught to read and write, were started. Although tuition was reduced at the state university, the institution was greatly improved by the addition of many new facilities, including major medical and dental schools. Rickety toll bridges were replaced with modern free bridges, and thousands of miles of new roads were paved, mainly in rural areas where farmers had found it difficult to send their products to market. New industries and more trade were attracted to the state, partly because of its better transportation system and also because the state's ports were enlarged and modernized.

When Long was determined to accomplish something, he insisted that his orders be carried out, no matter what tactics had to be used. He decided, for example, that he needed a lavish new governor's mansion in Baton Rouge, but some of his opponents in the legislature balked at spending the taxpayers' money for this expensive project. So Long, who liked to be known as "The Kingfish," gathered a small army of convicts from the state prison, led them to the old mansion, and personally supervised the destruction of the governor's house. Another time, when members of the legislature hesitated to appropriate funds for a new capitol building, Long had a hole drilled in the roof of the old statehouse so that rain would pour down on the head of one of the legislators who dared to criticize the governor's request. The Kingfish continued to bully the fearful legislators until he got a magnificent new capitol. Adorned with gleaming marble corridors, rich woods, and elegant furnishings, the new statehouse was topped by a thirty-four-story office tower that included Long's profile in bronze on the elevator doors.

Like most other dictators, Long was totally ruthless in striking down anyone who would not render him complete obedience. The slightest questioning of his commands caused the offenders—and often their relatives—to lose government jobs. On one occasion, when a Long supporter threatened to defect to the opposition shortly before an important election, the governor had him kidnapped and held on a remote island. During his confinement, the victim probably was offered some reward in return for his cooperation; when he was released, the man went on the radio to explain meekly that he had been kidnapped merely to protect him from his enemies.[3]

A Louisiana law limited the governor to one term in office, but this did not impede Long's political career. In 1930 he ran for a seat in the Senate and won the election easily. The Kingfish, however, served the rest of his term as governor because he did not want to step aside and let the lieutenant governor, a political opponent, head the state government. Long waited more than a year—until one of his loyal puppets was elected governor—before he assumed his seat in the Senate.

When Long finally moved to Washington, D.C., he

quickly made his presence known in the Senate. He got into a squabble with the other senator from Louisiana, who then refused to escort Long to the front of the Senate chamber to take his oath of office. Long fought with the Senate Democratic leader, Joseph Robinson of Arkansas, and resigned from the committees to which he had been appointed. Most newcomers say little on the floor during their first weeks in the Senate and quietly observe how to serve efficiently in that body—but not Huey Long. He immediately started to deliver long, rambling speeches that often contained nasty personal slurs aimed at other senators, shocking profanity, and crude bits of hillbilly humor. And when he opposed a bill strongly, he frequently resorted to the filibuster, a delaying tactic in which he talked endlessly in the hope that his colleagues finally would drop the bill and move on to other business.

Senator Long had his own plan for attacking the Depression—called the Share the Wealth Plan—and he took every opportunity to publicize it on the Senate floor, in newspaper stories, and on radio broadcasts. His plan called for new tax regulations that would place strict limits on the amount of wealth that Americans could own and pass on to their heirs. Each rich person could keep up to $1 million, but on every $1 million he or she owned over that amount there would be a sharply increasing tax that would reduce all fortunes to about $3 million. The government would confiscate all income that exceeded $1 million a year and seize all inheritances greater than $1 million.

According to the Share the Wealth Plan, the money taken from the rich people would be redistributed to the country's poor folk. From this fund, Long claimed that each needy family throughout the United States would receive a "homestead allowance" of five thousand dollars and an annual income of two thousand to twenty-five hundred dollars. Economists quickly pointed out that this plan was fatally flawed: even if the entire fortunes of all millionaires were confiscated, the money collected would be only a small fraction of the amount needed to provide the benefits that Long had promised.

Nevertheless, many Americans who had little income during the Depression climbed on the Kingfish's bandwagon. They were overjoyed by the Louisiana senator's plan to "soak the rich" and give the proceeds to impoverished families—without their having to do one day's work for their government handout. Share the Wealth clubs began sprouting all over the country, and Huey Long was becoming a national figure to be reckoned with.

When Franklin D. Roosevelt became president in 1933, Long at first supported the new leader in the White House. He was pleased that many of FDR's New Deal programs and agencies were intended to help the same people whose cause he championed, the victims of the Depression. But the Kingfish soon learned that the new president was much shrewder and far more capable than the stooges he had pushed around back home in Louisiana. Returning from an interview with Roosevelt, he confided to a close friend: "I found a man as smart as I am. I don't know if I can travel with him."[4] Soon, the southern senator began finding fault with bills FDR wanted Congress to pass, and he became outspokenly critical of the president's leadership.

Long sincerely believed that Roosevelt was moving far too slowly and cautiously in dealing with the nation's economic ills. But the widening rift between the two men developed more from a personal than a political clash. T. Harry Williams, Long's chief biographer, pointed out that the Kingfish definitely "could not be second . . . and therefore he had to break with Roosevelt. . . . The battle between them was waged in the Senate and in presidential press conferences and over the radio and in the press, and eventually it reached such epic proportions that it threatened to tear the Democratic party to pieces."[5]

FDR had reason to be deeply troubled by Long's growing political strength and vicious attacks on his administration. The president first tried to discipline the Louisiana

On the evening of April 14, 1865, President Abraham Lincoln
was shot at Ford's Theater in Washington by John Wilkes Booth,
shown here on the stage of the theater. The president died the
following morning.

Lincoln's burial at Oak Ridge Cemetery in Springfield, Illinois,
on May 4, 1865

President Andrew Johnson addressing citizens in Washington
in February 1866

Charles J. Guiteau shoots President Garfield, while Secretary of State Blaine stands amazed at right. One bullet lodged behind the spine and caused blood poisoning. Below, the wounded President's bedding is shifted at the White House. After suffering for weeks in the Washington heat, he was moved to the seashore at Elberon, New Jersey, where he died September 19. Garfield had been in wonderful spirits the day he was shot. In the morning his son ran into his room and made a flying leap across his bed. "*You* can't do that!" he cried, but the President jumped up in his nightshirt and did it. Then he got dressed and went off to catch a train for a reunion at Williams College, his alma mater.

Guiteau entertains the jury with a comic speech. His behavior suggested insanity.

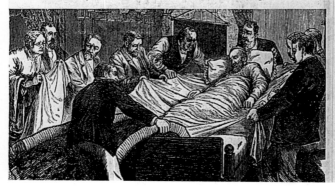

Guiteau hangs June 30, 1882. His skeleton went to the Army Medical Museum.

Messengers conveyed the official bulletin to members of the cabinet that President James Garfield had been shot.

Above: Chester Alan Arthur succeeded Garfield in the presidency. He is
shown here at the ceremony opening the Brooklyn Bridge in 1883.
Facing page, top: President William McKinley being shot by
Leon Czolgosz at the Pan-American Exposition in Buffalo,
New York, on September 6, 1901. He died eight days later.
Czolgosz was tried, convicted, and sentenced to death.
Facing page, bottom: The observation car of the funeral train
in which McKinley's casket was transported to his
hometown of Canton, Ohio, for burial.

Theodore Roosevelt became the country's youngest chief
executive after McKinley died.

Senator Huey Long of Louisiana (left) and Norman Thomas, a leading spokesman for socialism in America, meet for a debate in 1934.

One of the most outspoken, powerful radicals in American history, Long excited people wherever he went. Shown here in New Orleans in 1935 (center, with hat in hand) after a return from Washington, Long is greeted by a crowd of American Legion and Veterans of Foreign Wars members. Long led the unsuccessful fight to override President Franklin D. Roosevelt's veto of a soldier's bonus bill.

Above: John F. Kennedy and his wife, Jacqueline, ride in a ticker tape parade in New York City.
Right: Two brothers—both to be struck down by assassins' bullets within four and a half years of each other. President John F. Kennedy (right) and his brother Attorney General Robert Kennedy confer at the White House in October 1962.

Right: Lee Harvey Oswald, charged with the assassination of President Kennedy. He was never brought to trial—Oswald was shot to death by Jack Ruby two days after Kennedy was killed. Controversy exists to this day about whether Oswald acted alone or was part of a conspiracy to assassinate the president. *Below:* Kennedy's body lies in state at the Capitol Rotunda on November 24, 1963. His young daughter, Caroline, kneels by the casket.

President Lyndon B. Johnson after
taking office carried forth many
of the slain Kennedy's programs.

Martin Luther King, Jr., (on right at front of line) leads a long line of chanting black demonstrators during a march on city hall in Birmingham, Alabama, on April 12, 1963. (Ralph Abernathy is on King's left.) King launched a major civil rights campaign in Birmingham, a city he believed to be the most segregated in the United States.

Dr. King grasps the outstretched hands of a welcoming crowd as his motorcade moved through the streets of Baltimore in October 1964. King was on a six-city tour to encourage urban blacks to vote in the upcoming national election.

Protesting America's involvement in Vietnam during the late 1960s, King was joined here by other antiwar protesters during the greatest demonstration ever held against the war in Vietnam. This event took place in New York City in 1967—some 200,000 people marched toward the United Nations where Nobel Peace Prize winner Dr. King addressed the crowd.

On April 4, 1968, Martin Luther King, Jr., was shot by James Earl Ray (second from right, wearing muddy clothes) in Memphis. Ray was convicted and sentenced to ninety-nine years in prison.

As attorney general in his brother's administration,
Robert Kennedy's most significant contributions were in
the area of civil rights. Here, Kennedy (second from left)
greets delegates to the NAACP convention in Washington
in June 1964. The delegates marched in silent protest
over the disappearance of three young civil rights
workers in Mississippi. (The boy in the center of the
photo is ten-year-old Darrell Evers, whose father,
Medgar Evers, was killed by a sniper's bullet in
Jackson, Mississippi, in 1963.)

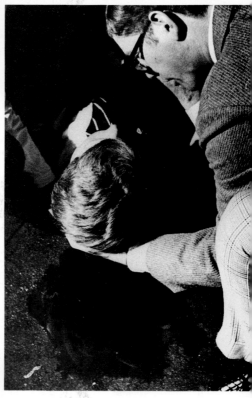

A beaming Senator
Robert F. Kennedy is
surrounded by supporters as
he makes a victory
statement after winning
the California presidential
primary on June 4, 1968.
Minutes later, shortly after
midnight, he was struck by
an assassin's bullet.
He died the next day.
Bobby Kennedy was buried
in Arlington National
Cemetery near his brother,
President John F. Kennedy.

Sirhan Sirhan was convicted
of killing Robert Kennedy and
was sentenced to death.
However, that sentence
was reduced to life
imprisonment when the
Supreme Court ruled in
1972 that the death
penalty was unconstitutional.

senator by refusing to consult him before appointing federal officeholders in his state. But this only increased the senator's wrath, and he stepped up his campaign against the White House, even charging that Postmaster General James A. Farley, a close friend of Roosevelt's, had been involved in shady deals. Meanwhile, the president was flooded with appeals from irate Louisiana citizens who wanted the national government to take firm steps against the illegal activities and corruption of the Long political machine that still controlled their state. In September 1934, the president considered the idea of sending federal troops into Louisiana to enforce that section of the Constitution that guarantees to every state "a republican form of government," but he rejected this possibility because it seemed too rash and explosive.[6]

Meanwhile, the Share the Wealth movement was expanding rapidly. "Every Man a King" became a household slogan that many poor families repeated again and again. (Long also used it as the title of his autobiography, which was published in 1933.) The Kingfish boasted, in February 1935, that there were twenty-seven thousand Share the Wealth clubs and he had a mailing list of more than 7.5 million supporters. These figures may have been exaggerated, but there was no doubt that the Kingfish had large armies of ardent, even fanatic, disciples in many parts of the country. Long hoped and probably expected that these legions of devoted followers would form the vanguard of a massive poor people's campaign to win him the presidency. He believed that the highest office in the land was within his grasp. In the spring of 1935, he even wrote the rough draft of a book titled *My First Days in the White House*, which was polished by journalists and published later that same year.

A secret poll taken by the Democratic National Committee in 1935 showed that if Long ran on a third-party ticket in the 1936 presidential election, he might poll 3 or 4 million votes. Since most of these votes would come from

Democrats, Roosevelt feared that Long's candidacy might divide the Democratic party so badly that his Republican opponent could win the election.[7]

In the spring of 1935, Roosevelt launched a series of new programs that constituted what has been called the "Second New Deal." They stole some of Huey Long's thunder by dealing directly with many of the specific problems that the Louisiana senator had publicized. To help the unemployed, the Works Progress Administration (WPA) was established, and it gave jobs to over 3 million people. To provide benefits for elderly and physically disabled Americans, Social Security was started. The right of workers to join unions and bargain collectively was strengthened by the National Labor Relations Act. And to help reduce the concentration of wealth in the hands of the upper economic class, Congress passed legislation that raised taxes on yearly incomes above fifty thousand dollars and imposed inheritance taxes of up to 70 percent on large estates. These and other New Deal measures certainly were less radical than the Share the Wealth Plan, but they showed the public that the man in the White House was developing new ways to improve the standard of living for millions of Americans.

Long returned to Baton Rouge during the congressional recess in the summer of 1935. Even though he no longer held a state office, the Kingfish still ruled Louisiana as if it were his personal kingdom, and he continued eliminating enemies who would not be dominated by his political machine. Judge Benjamin Pavy of Louisiana's Thirteenth Judicial District was one of the men whom the Long organization had not been able to control. This infuriated the Kingfish, who ordered that Pavy's brother, a school principal, and his daughter, a teacher, both be fired. Then, on September 7, Long had the state legislature redraw the boundaries of the Thirteenth Judicial District in a way that made it nearly impossible for Judge Pavy to win reelection because his new district fell in an area firmly controlled by Long's supporters.

The following evening, a tall, thin, bespectacled young man entered the capitol building with a concealed .32 caliber pistol. He was Dr. Carl Austin Weiss, Jr., a soft-spoken, respected physician, and the son-in-law of Judge Pavy. Shortly after nine o'clock, Long left the House chamber and walked rapidly down a corridor. Suddenly Weiss stepped out from behind a pillar, raised his right hand, aimed his small pistol at Long's rib cage, and fired. Long screamed, clutched his abdomen, and staggered down the hallway. His bodyguards wrestled Weiss to the floor and, even after fatally wounding him with shots that tore through his face, neck, and torso, continued to riddle his body with bullets.

Huey Long died two days later. After the largest funeral ever held in Louisiana, he was buried in front of the skyscraper capitol that he had built.

The motive that led Weiss to murder Long has never been fully established. Before the crime, he had seemed to be a stable, law-abiding, well-liked person, with no history of mental illness or police record. But Weiss had demonstrated a deep devotion to his entire family, including his in-laws. Apparently he had been strongly angered by Long's continual abuse of the Pavys, and the redrawing of his father-in-law's judicial district to force him out of office was the final straw that triggered Weiss to assassinate the senator.

After Long's death, Gerald L. K. Smith, his chief lieutenant, tried to keep the Share the Wealth movement afloat, but his efforts were futile. In the 1936 presidential election, Smith pleaded with Long's followers to support Representative William Lemke of North Dakota, who was the candidate of the radical Union party. But this new third party made a dismal showing at the polls, garnering fewer than 900,000 votes of more than 45 million cast. As a political force, the Share the Wealth movement had been stripped of its vitality when its founder and dynamic leader was laid to rest.

While he was governor of Louisiana, Huey Long

brought some long overdue benefits to many people in his state. Later, as a senator, he helped focus national attention on the plight of millions of Americans who were suffering from the devastating effects of the Great Depression. And the growing popularity of this outspoken crusader may have been an important factor in prodding President Roosevelt to propose—and Congress to enact into law—major relief and reform measures in 1935.

On the other hand, Long and his political machine represented a serious threat to the democratic principles on which our country was founded. In Louisiana, he was not content until he had assumed the role of a dictator with all the power needed to crush his political enemies. On the national stage, his lust for power posed an even more ominous danger. Rexford G. Tugwell, one of Roosevelt's main advisers, said the president feared that if the New Deal failed to solve the problems of capitalism, restless radicals might erupt into some kind of revolution under Long's leadership.[8]

Huey Long was a prime example of a *demagogue*, a leader who appeals to the emotions and prejudices of people primarily to advance his own political career. What would this demagogue have done if an assassin's bullet had not silenced his strident voice when he was only forty-three years of age? No one can answer this question, but it is most unlikely that the Kingfish would have been a mere spectator sitting quietly on the sidelines and watching other politicians perform on center stage.

JOHN F. KENNEDY

The End
of
Camelot

John F. Kennedy's first political target was the seat in the United States House of Representatives from the Eleventh Congressional District in Massachusetts. That race took place in 1946, the year after World War II ended. Kennedy was only twenty-eight years old when he launched his campaign to become a member of Congress.

The Eleventh District, located mainly in East Boston, was largely composed of blue-collar, working-class voters. Ten candidates ran for the Democratic nomination. When they were introduced at political rallies, the other nine candidates often reminded Bostonians that they had "come up the hard way." But when young Jack Kennedy took his turn at the microphone, he smiled wryly and candidly admitted, "I'm the one who didn't come up the hard way."[1]

Kennedy enjoyed more advantages than his opponents could claim. He belonged to one of America's wealthiest families and never had the need to earn money. As a child and teenager, Jack attended prestigious private schools, and he graduated with honors from Harvard University. Handsome and robust, he excelled at sports and, in spite of being somewhat shy, made friends easily. Among his many talents was the ability to write and speak gracefully and fluently. Kennedy also was a World War II hero: his courageous actions in the South Pacific earned him a Purple Heart and the Navy and Marine Corps medal.

Jack was the second of nine children in a large family that had long been involved in politics. His maternal grandfather, John F. (Honey Fitz) Fitzgerald, had been a congressman and later the mayor of Boston. His paternal grandfather, Patrick J. Kennedy, served in both houses of the Massachusetts state legislature. During Franklin D. Roosevelt's administration, Joseph P. Kennedy, Jack's father, was appointed chairman of the newly created Securities and Exchange Commission in 1934, and from 1937 to 1940 he was ambassador to Great Britain. Jack spent the second college semester of his junior year as secretary to his father in London, and when he returned to Harvard he wrote his senior thesis on Britain's disarmament and appeasement policy after World War I. Published in 1940 under the title *Why England Slept*, his senior thesis became a book that earned its youthful author about forty thousand dollars in royalties.

When Jack first entered the race for a Massachusetts seat in Congress, he was accused of being a carpetbagger because his family had lived the previous twenty years in New York City. But the Kennedy clan met this challenge with an energetic whirlwind campaign that took Boston by storm. Grandfather Honey Fitz enlisted the aid of many old cronies. The attractive Kennedy women, mother and sisters, staged campaign parties throughout the district and passed out thousands of brochures calling for Jack's election. Brother Bobby, only twenty years old, appealed for votes in those difficult areas where Jack faced his toughest opposition. Jack got in touch with some of his Navy buddies, who traveled to Boston and praised the candidate's wartime service. And Jack could count on his rich father to pay many of the campaign costs.

Kennedy won the Democratic primary by a two-to-one margin over his nearest rival, and he easily defeated his Republican opponent in the general election. He was re-elected twice to the House of Representatives. Congressman Kennedy compiled a moderate liberal voting record. He opposed the conservative Taft-Hartley labor bill, and he strongly favored low-cost public housing, even denouncing the American Legion for its opposition to federal aid for housing. In foreign affairs, he supported two measures that helped European nations, the Truman Doctrine and the Marshall Plan, but he blamed the Truman administration for contributing to the loss of China to the Communists in 1949.

After spending six years in the House of Representatives, Kennedy decided to run for the United States Senate in 1952. To win a seat in the upper house of Congress, he had to oust the popular Republican incumbent, Henry Cabot Lodge II. Moreover, 1952 appeared to be a banner year for Republicans, whose presidential ticket was headed by the widely respected World War II general Dwight D. Eisenhower. Kennedy campaigned strenuously, and he became one of the few Democrats to buck the Republican trend—he defeated Lodge by about 70,000 votes, while Eisenhower was carrying Massachusetts by more than 200,000 votes. Senator Kennedy was soon hailed as one of the most promising Democrats on the national scene, and he was reelected in 1958 with 74 percent of the vote.

During his first year in the Senate, Kennedy married Jacqueline (Jackie) Bouvier, the beautiful twenty-four-year-old daughter of a socially prominent family. Jackie had studied at the Sorbonne in Paris (she spoke French fluently) and was graduated from George Washington University in 1951. At the time that she met Jack, she was a newspaper photographer. The Kennedys had two children, Caroline and John, Jr., and a third child who died shortly after birth.

In the Senate, Kennedy helped pass several bills that were important to the textile industry in Massachusetts, and he sponsored measures that improved his state's conservation program. He was the only Massachusetts legislator to vote in favor of developing the St. Lawrence Seaway, a project intended to divert merchant ships from Atlantic Coast ports to inland cities on the Great Lakes. One of the several Senate committees on which Kennedy served investigated improper activities in labor-management relations. His younger brother Robert was the chief legal counsel for this committee. The two Kennedys drew nationwide public attention when they investigated racketeering among prominent labor union officials.

Through his years in Congress, Jack Kennedy was plagued by a painful back, and by the summer of 1954 he could get about only on crutches. (He had suffered a back injury while playing football in college, and the condition was aggravated by a second injury when he was in the Navy.) In October 1954, Kennedy had spinal fusion surgery, which was followed by an acute infection that was almost fatal. The Massachusetts senator hovered so near death that he was given the last rites of the Catholic church, but he slowly rallied.

Several months later a second operation was performed, which was only partially successful. Kennedy's condition never was completely cured, and he endured a severe backache for the rest of his life. While recuperating from his second surgery, Kennedy wrote, with the assistance of aides, a book titled *Profiles in Courage*. It told the story of politicians who had put principles ahead of popularity, and it was awarded a Pulitzer Prize.

At the 1956 Democratic party convention, Adlai Stevenson won the nomination for the presidency and then surprised the delegates by telling them to choose any vice presidential candidate they wanted. A frenzied scramble ensued, and on the first ballot thirteen names, including John Kennedy's, were placed in nomination. Kennedy spurted into the lead on the second ballot and came within forty votes of being selected as Stevenson's running mate. But after the roll call, enough state delegations switched their votes to Senator Estes Kefauver of Tennessee to give him the nomination. At the polls, Stevenson and Kefauver were defeated in a landslide by the Republican ticket of incumbents Dwight D. Eisenhower and Richard Nixon. It was a blessing in disguise for Kennedy's political future that he had not been part of the Democrats' losing ticket.

Four years later, Kennedy sought the presidential nomination of the Democratic party. To achieve this goal, he realized that he had to overcome three major obstacles: his youth, his family's enormous wealth, and his Catholicism (no Catholic had ever been president). Since Kennedy had to prove that he could be a large vote getter outside Massachusetts, he entered Democratic primary elections in seven states scattered across the country. The key primary was in West Virginia, where only 5 percent of the population was Catholic. The Massachusetts senator carried West Virginia with 61 percent of the vote, and he swept to victory in all the other states in which his name was on the ballot and in three more states where he was a write-in candidate. Kennedy won the Democratic presidential nomination, amassing nearly twice as many delegate votes as those cast for his nearest rival, Senate Majority Leader Lyndon B. Johnson of Texas.

Kennedy then asked Johnson to be his running mate, surprising the convention and disappointing many liberals, who regarded Johnson as a southerner with more conservative views than Kennedy's. It was even more surprising that Johnson accepted the nomination; few delegates believed that the Texan would give up the vast power he wielded as Senate majority leader to seek the almost powerless vice presidency.

The Republicans selected as their presidential nominee Vice President Richard Nixon of California. Like Kennedy, Nixon had first been elected to the House of Representatives in 1946 and later served in the Senate. In 1952, Nixon won the vice presidency on the ticket headed by Eisenhower, and four years later he was reelected. One exciting new development in the 1960 presidential race was that Nixon and Kennedy agreed to hold four nationally televised debates—the first time in history that television covered debates between presidential candidates. Among the millions of viewers who watched the initial debate, it generally was agreed that Kennedy gave the better performance. He appeared more poised, self-assured, and decisive than Nixon, and this debate helped dispel the notion that he was too young and immature to hold the highest office in the land.

Kennedy also needed to put an end to the doubts held by large numbers of non-Catholics regarding whether he could prevent his private religious views from interfering with the public decisions he would make if elected president. The Democratic nominee met this issue head-on in a notable speech to a large gathering of Protestant ministers in Houston, Texas. In this address, he declared himself in favor of the absolute separation of church and state and pledged that as president he would make all his decisions "without regard to outside religious pressures or dictates."[2] Many—but not all—voters now were convinced that Kennedy's religion was no longer an important issue.

The election results were extremely close; never before or since in the twentieth century has the margin of victory been so narrow in the popular vote. Of nearly 69 million votes cast, Kennedy defeated Nixon by 114,673 votes. In the electoral vote, Kennedy led 303 to 219, but he won eleven states by less than 51 percent of the vote. Without the help of vice presidential candidate Johnson, Kennedy almost certainly would have been denied the White House. The Senate majority leader's appeal to voters in the South and Southwest played a large part in obtaining slim victories for the Democratic ticket in Texas, New Mexico, Arkansas, Louisiana, North Carolina, and South Carolina.

Inauguration day was bitterly cold and snow was blanketing the ground in Washington, D.C., when forty-three-year-old John F. Kennedy—the youngest American ever elected president—took the oath of office. He told the crowd gathered at his inauguration, "Let the word go forth from this time and place to friend and foe alike, that the torch has been passed to a new generation of Americans."[3] As he had indicated in his Inaugural Address, the new president vibrated with the boundless energy of youth, and other government officials were expected to keep pace with him. Secretary of Labor Arthur J. Goldberg said that Kennedy acted as if "the deadline for everything is day before yesterday."[4]

Perhaps the most famous statement in Kennedy's Inaugural Address was "Ask not what your country can do for you; ask what you can do for your country."[5] Some Americans responded to this challenge by joining the Peace Corps, which the new president established shortly after he took office. This agency of the State Department enlisted volunteers to teach and provide technical assistance to people in underdeveloped countries. About eighty-five thousand Americans, mostly young adults, served in the corps over the next twenty years.

In the same month that he started the Peace Corps, January 1961, Kennedy proposed the Alliance for Progress to raise the standard of living in the impoverished countries of Latin America. Later that year at Punta del Este, Uruguay, representatives of the United States and nineteen Latin American nations signed the Alianza agreement, which focused attention on agrarian and tax reforms. The United States launched the Alliance for Progress with a promise to spend $10 billion in aid to its southern neighbors over a period of ten years.

President Kennedy had been in office less than three months when his administration faced its first international crisis. While Eisenhower was still in the White House, the U.S. Central Intelligence Agency (CIA) had devised a plan to overthrow the Communist regime of Fidel Castro. It involved about fifteen hundred Cuban exiles who had fled their homeland and were eager for an opportunity to drive Castro from power. Many of the exiles had been trained, mainly in Guatemala, by the CIA, and they were armed with American weapons. Their goal was to invade Cuba at Bahia de los Cochinos (Bay of Pigs) and secure a fortified beachhold on the shore; their landing was expected to spark a spontaneous uprising by the Cuban people that would topple their Communist dictator.

Kennedy felt that the mission must go ahead as planned during the Eisenhower administration, but it failed dismally to accomplish its purpose. When the guerrilla fighters reached the Cuban shore, Castro's soldiers and tanks provided overwhelmingly strong opposition. When this happened, some of the president's advisers urged him to unleash an air attack on Cuba and send massive United States naval forces to help the stranded invaders. But JFK (the first president since Franklin D. Roosevelt that the press often identified by his initials) steadfastly refused to enlarge the military operation. After a few days of fierce fighting, Castro's forces repelled the invaders with heavy loss of life. No uprising on the island against Castro's rule occurred, and about eleven hundred guerrillas were taken as prisoners. (The following year the United States paid $53 million in food and medical supplies for their release.) Kennedy accepted full responsibility for the mission's failure, but after this embarrassing episode his popularity actually climbed in the polls—indicating that Americans tend to rally behind their president during times when there is trouble with a foreign country.

In June 1961, Kennedy held a summit meeting with Nikita Khrushchev, in Vienna. The Soviet premier used this occasion to try to intimidate the young, untested American president, whose experience in international affairs had been limited to the Bay of Pigs fiasco. Khrushchev boasted that his country's industrial growth was higher than

America's, that the Soviets now had their own hydrogen bombs, that they led Americans in the development of both ballistic missiles and conventional arms, and that they were far ahead of the United States in the conquest of outer space. The Soviet premier hailed communism as the wave of the future and predicted that it would wipe out "American imperialism" throughout Latin America, Asia, and Africa.

The future of Berlin was the most critical issue discussed by the two world leaders. West Berlin, a free and democratic city, lay entirely within the boundaries of East Germany, an area that the Soviet Union had occupied in World War II and controlled after the war. Khrushchev threatened to sign a separate peace treaty with East Germany, thereby permitting that new country to seal off all access routes from Western non-Communist countries to West Berlin. He thundered at Kennedy that any nation that dared to "violate" East Germany's travel restrictions would be creating another "Sarajevo" that could lead to a third world war. Kennedy angrily replied that the freedom of West Berlin would be defended at all costs. (In August 1961, the Communists erected the Berlin Wall to prevent East Berliners from escaping into West Berlin. Nearly two years later, President Kennedy stood at that wall and told a wildly cheering crowd in West Berlin, "All free men, wherever they live, are citizens of Berlin, and, therefore, as a free man, I take pride in the words *Ich bin ein Berliner* [I am a Berliner].")[6]

The Soviet Union intensified the cold war in September 1961 by exploding a nuclear bomb in the atmosphere; this ended a thirty-four-month suspension of atomic weapons tests by the world's nuclear powers. The Soviets continued their testing, detonating at least fifty nuclear devices over the next two months, including a hydrogen device of fifty megatons, the most powerful yet exploded. President Kennedy strongly criticized the Soviet resumption of testing and struck back by declaring that the United States also would begin testing its nuclear devices again, but at that time he specified that the American tests would be underground, where they would create no fallout. The president then tried to persuade the Soviets to agree to a test-ban treaty, but Khrushchev refused JFK's offer. When the Soviet Union persisted with atmospheric testing, in April 1962 Kennedy reluctantly ordered the United States to resume its testing of nuclear weapons in the atmosphere, but he was concerned about the potentially dangerous effect of poisoning the atmosphere.

The American president also sought to prevent the United States from falling behind the Soviet Union in human space flight. In April 1961, a Soviet astronaut achieved the world's first manned orbital flight. This prompted President Kennedy to appear before Congress and ask for a firm commitment to spend the enormous funds needed for an advanced space program that would place Americans on the moon before the end of the decade. The next month, the Navy commander Alan Shepard, Jr., became the first American to travel in a space capsule, reaching an altitude of 116 miles. Less than one year later, in February 1962, another American astronaut, Lt. Col. John Glenn, Jr., made a thrilling voyage into space, orbiting the earth three times within five hours. (The crowning achievement in human space flight occurred in July 1969 when Neil Armstrong and Edwin Aldrin became the first men to walk on the moon, four days after the launching of *Apollo XI*.)

The most serious international crisis during the Kennedy presidency occurred in October 1962 when American U-2 planes photographed Soviet offensive missile bases in Cuba. Missiles launched from these bases would be capable of striking two-thirds of the United States and many areas in Latin America. Photos showed that sixteen, and possibly thirty-two, missile sites would be ready for firing within a week. It was feared that nuclear weapons propelled from these sites could kill 80 million Americans.

Declaring that such missiles posed a grave threat to our

national security, President Kennedy issued a stern ultimatum to Premier Khrushchev that this nuclear menace must be ended immediately. He warned that any attack from Cuba would be regarded as an attack by the Soviet Union, and the United States would retaliate against both Cuba and the Soviet nation.

Some of Kennedy's advisers urged an immediate air strike against Cuba; others proposed a naval blockade to prevent the Soviets from shipping more missiles to Cuba, coupled with a demand that all nuclear weapons be removed from the island and the missile sites be dismantled. The president chose the blockade alternative; it had the advantage of giving the Soviets an opportunity to back down without bloodshed. Kennedy reported his decision to quarantine Cuba in a somber television broadcast on Monday, October 22.

The stage was thus set for a possible confrontation between the two superpowers that could have been the opening salvo of World War III. American warships sped to their stations in a large arc five hundred miles out to sea from the eastern tip of Cuba. American airplanes carrying nuclear bombs were ordered on war alert. The entire world waited tensely as Soviet ships moved across the Atlantic Ocean toward Cuba. On Wednesday, October 24, the first group of these ships bearing missiles turned aside before reaching the U.S. naval blockade. "We're eyeball to eyeball," observed Secretary of State Dean Rusk, "and I think the other fellow just blinked."[7]

A few days later, Khrushchev agreed to dismantle the missile sites and retrieve the nuclear weapons from Cuba in return for a pledge by the United States not to invade Cuba. By the end of November, the Soviets had fulfilled their promise, the Americans had lifted the blockade, and the ominous crisis had ended.

President Kennedy instructed his advisers not to gloat about the stunning American diplomatic victory that had just taken place. He felt that Khrushchev's willingness to act in a restrained manner regarding the Cuban missiles might be an indication that the Soviet premier could now be persuaded to drop his opposition to a nuclear test-ban agreement. The president wrote Khrushchev a letter, saying, "I think we should give priority to questions relating to the proliferation [rapid spread] of nuclear weapons, on earth and outer space, and to the great effort for a nuclear test ban."[8]

Khrushchev was slow in responding to Kennedy's request, but finally in July 1963 representatives of the Soviet Union, the United States, and Great Britain signed a limited nuclear test-ban treaty. It prohibited nuclear-weapon testing in the atmosphere, outer space, and the oceans, but not underground. Eventually the treaty was agreed to by more than one hundred nations, and the fear of nuclear fallout was greatly reduced. President Kennedy hailed the nuclear test-ban treaty as a "victory for mankind" and considered it one of the most outstanding achievements of his administration.

President Kennedy also was concerned about the deteriorating situation in South Vietnam, where the anti-Communist government of the dictator Ngo Dinh Diem was then locked in a struggle against Communist guerrillas who came to be called the Viet Cong. The United States began sending limited help to the South Vietnamese government during the Eisenhower administration—about eight hundred U.S. military advisers and $300 million a year in military aid. While Kennedy was in the White House, the Viet Cong, aided by the Communist government of North Vietnam, increased its attacks against the Diem regime and occupied several rural areas. President Kennedy hoped that South Vietnam would not fall to the Communists, as China had a few years after World War II, so he approved more financial aid to that beleaguered country and increased the number of U.S. military advisers stationed there to sixteen thousand. But Kennedy vetoed proposals by some of his advisers to commit American troops to fighting in South Vietnam, and shortly before his death he spoke about limiting American help in the war.

Kennedy was an active president on the domestic front, as well as in foreign affairs. To combat inflation, he used his influence to set up voluntary wage-price guidelines intended to prevent sharp increases in workers' wages and also in prices that industries charged for their products. In March 1962, steelworkers signed a contract without a wage increase, but a short time later several steel companies announced increases in their prices. Kennedy was angered by this action. He applied strong pressure against the steel companies and threatened lawsuits. Within a few days, the price increases were canceled.

The Kennedy administration sent to Congress a large number of proposals dealing with a wide variety of subjects. Of the 107 recommendations that it made to Congress in the first two years of JFK's presidency, 73 were enacted into law. Congressional approval was given to larger Social Security benefits, a higher minimum wage, and aid to economically depressed areas in the country. One of Kennedy's major legislative successes was the passage of the Trade Expansion Act in 1962. It gave the president broad powers to lower tariffs substantially, thereby helping the United States trade with other countries on equal terms.

Congress, however, rejected some of Kennedy's most important proposals. Medicare—the plan calling for government financial aid to help pay the costs of elderly persons' medical bills—was turned down in the Senate by a fifty-two to forty-eight vote. When this occurred, the president went on television to tell the nation that the failure of Congress to pass the Medicare measure was a "most serious defeat for every American family."[9] Another proposal advanced by JFK would have cut taxes in order to stimulate the economy and would have closed some unfair tax loopholes, but Congress did not pass this tax bill during his administration.

One of the country's most pressing problems during the

1960s was the need to extend to blacks and other minorities all of the civil rights that were enjoyed by other American citizens. While Kennedy was president, the executive department of the federal government took significant steps to reduce racial discrimination. On several occasions, civil rights demonstrators in the South were protected by federal marshals, and successful campaigns were waged against some southern universities that previously had refused to admit blacks. The Kennedy administration's achievements in the field of civil rights were due primarily to the zeal and courage demonstrated by Attorney General Robert F. Kennedy, the president's brother, who headed the Department of Justice (see Chapter 7).

Violence erupted in April and May 1963 in Birmingham, Alabama, where civil rights activists led by the Reverend Martin Luther King, Jr., protested segregation in that city (see Chapter 6). More than 750 demonstrations, affecting nearly every major city with a large black population, took place in the ten weeks after the outbreak of unrest in Birmingham. President Kennedy responded to the mounting civil rights crisis by demanding a comprehensive bill passed by Congress to ensure blacks the rights of citizenship guaranteed them by the Constitution. This bill would, among other things, provide equal access for blacks in all places of "public accommodation," such as hotels, restaurants, theaters, and restrooms. It would give the attorney general greater authority in bringing suits against segregated school systems. Finally, this civil rights bill would strengthen the legal procedures already in existence to assure job equality and voting rights for blacks.

President Kennedy delivered a televised message on the civil rights issue on June 11, 1963. He asked the American public, ". . . are we to say to the world, and much more importantly, to each other that this is a land of the free except for the Negroes; that we have no second-class citizens except Negroes?"[10] The president clearly spelled out, "Now the time has come for the nation to fulfill its promise. . . . It is time to act in the Congress, in your state and local legislative body, and, above all, in our lives."[11] JFK's civil rights bill became a hotly debated subject in Congress. Some southern legislators felt that it went too far in changing long-standing traditions, and they blocked passage of the bill. This bitterly disappointed the president.

Aside from the policies he launched, the orders he issued, and the legislation he sponsored, something else about John F. Kennedy captured the minds and hearts of the American people. Much like Franklin D. Roosevelt three decades before, Kennedy had a remarkable ability to reach out to people and fill them with hope. Citizens throughout the land were drawn to this youthful Irish-American by his boundless vigor and vitality, his wit as well as his wisdom, his tremendous charisma and gracious style, and, most of all, his steadfast optimism. This optimism was contagious, and young people especially seemed more confident because they trusted the man in the White House, who was their hero and, for many, their role model.

The public was captivated by the president's large, attractive family, including his glamorous, talented wife Jackie. Newspapers and magazine articles told about Mrs. Kennedy's redecorating the White House, and the splendid social affairs that were held there to honor great musicians, artists, and authors. Other stories told about the Kennedy clan's roughing up each other in touch-football games at their family compound in Hyannis Port, Massachusetts, and about Jack and Jackie's receiving tumultuous welcomes wherever they traveled abroad, whether to sophisticated cities like Paris and Berlin or to rural communities in Jack's ancestral Irish homeland.

The American people—and, to a large extent, people everywhere in the free world—had a love affair with the dynamic chief executive, who was many years younger than most heads of state. When JFK was elected president in 1960, he won a little less than 50 percent of the popular vote, but pollsters found that in June 1963, when he had been in office about two and one-half years, 59 percent of the people claimed they had voted for him. After his death, the figure jumped to 65 percent, "meaning that over ten million voters had edited their memories."[12] The Kennedys won the affection of so many people that they were even likened to a royal family living in the magical legendary kingdom of King Arthur's Camelot. So when John F. Kennedy was cruelly struck down in Dallas on November 22, 1963, that event marked more than the untimely death of a popular president—it shattered the wondrous image of an American Camelot.

The president had gone with his wife to Dallas to make a political address at a luncheon. The Kennedys traveled with Governor and Mrs. John Connally of Texas through the city streets in an open limousine. As the motorcade proceeded, people lined the sidewalks ten to twelve deep, applauding warmly. Mrs. Connally turned to Kennedy and said, "Mr. President, you can't say Dallas doesn't love you."[13] Moments later, just as JFK's car passed a tall building called the Texas School Book Depository, shots rang out. The president, fatally shot through the head and throat, slumped into his wife's lap. Governor Connally also was seriously wounded, but he later recovered. The limousine raced to a nearby hospital, where President Kennedy was pronounced dead about a half-hour after the shooting.

A reporter, glancing up when he heard the crackle of gunfire, said he saw a rifle in a sixth-story window of the textbook depository. Shortly after the shooting, the description of a man seen suddenly leaving the textbook warehouse went out over the police radio. Patrolman J. D. Tippit stopped and started questioning a man who seemed to fit the description. The suspect fired his gun three times at Tippit, killing him instantly, and then fled on foot. In less than half an hour, the Dallas police captured Lee Harvey Oswald in a motion-picture theater, where he had hidden after allegedly murdering the president and Officer Tippit.

Oswald was a twenty-four-year-old former Marine. Authorities learned that he was a professed Communist who had lived for a time in the Soviet Union and that he was a supporter of the Cuban dictator, Fidel Castro. At the time of Kennedy's assassination, he was employed at the Texas School Book Depository, and it was discovered that he had purchased through the mail the type of rifle that ballistic tests showed could have been used to kill the president.

Oswald denied that he had murdered Kennedy, but he was never brought to trial. On Sunday, November 24, as he was being led across the basement of the city prison for transfer to another prison facility, Oswald was shot to death by Jack Ruby, a Dallas nightclub owner. Ruby never gave any rational explanation for killing Oswald and claimed that it was an act of wild impulse motivated by anger at the president's assassin.

One week after Kennedy died, the new president, Lyndon B. Johnson, created a commission to investigate and report on the facts relating to the tragedy. Supreme Court Chief Justice Earl Warren was appointed chairman. The Warren Commission conducted an intensive ten-month investigation, heard 552 witnesses, and produced a report in September 1964 that filled 26 volumes and included thousands of pages. The commission concluded that the shots that killed President Kennedy and wounded Governor Connally were fired by Oswald. It also declared that, on the basis of the evidence presented, it appeared that Oswald had acted alone.

The Warren Report, however, failed to answer conclusively many questions about the assassination. How many shots were fired at Kennedy? Did one of the bullets that hit Kennedy also strike Connally? Was there a second gunman? (Evidence suggested that one or more shots could have come from a grassy knoll in front of the presidential limousine.) Was it Oswald or someone impersonating him who fired the rifle from the textbook depository? If Oswald was guilty, what were his reasons for committing the crime? Was the murderer (or murderers) acting alone or as part of a conspiracy? If the assassination was plotted by a conspiracy, who were the conspirators and why did they want to kill the popular president?

In the years after Kennedy's death, attacks on the Warren Report increased. Congress in 1979 appointed a new commission to investigate the assassination. It made use of new acoustical analyses and other recent technology that had not been available to the Warren Commission in 1964. The 1979 commission agreed with the Warren Report that Oswald did fire three shots. But an acoustical analysis of sounds picked up at the scene by a motorcycle policeman's radio strongly indicated that a fourth shot had been fired, probably by a second assassin stationed on the grassy knoll. The new commission disputed the Warren Report's conclusion that Oswald had acted alone. It concluded that Kennedy probably was assassinated as the result of a conspiracy. The conspirators who masterminded the murder may have been members of an organized crime syndicate (it was discovered that Oswald had ties to a powerful underworld figure), or followers of Castro who wanted to strike down the American president in retaliation for alleged attempts by the CIA to eliminate the Cuban dictator. The conspiracy theory, however, has never been proved absolutely.

Shortly after Lyndon B. Johnson assumed the presidency, he addressed Congress and pledged his complete support for Kennedy's proposals that still had not been enacted into laws. He told the lawmakers that it was "a time for action" and that the late president's memory could best be honored by passing the bills that Kennedy had supported. Before he had become JFK's vice president, Johnson had been one of the most successful majority leaders in Senate history. He had demonstrated exceptional skills of persuasion in coaxing his colleagues to vote for or against measures that reached the Senate floor. Now, as president, he applied the same persuasive skills to the Kennedy program and helped push through Congress major bills that had languished while JFK was in the White House. One of these measures was a multibillion-dollar tax cut that Johnson signed into law on February 26, 1964. Another was Medicare, enacted in 1965, which provided medical benefits for most persons sixty-five years of age and older.

President Johnson's most outstanding legislative achievements were in the field of civil rights. The 1964 Civil Rights Act, which had been originally proposed by President Kennedy but turned down by Congress, was the most far-reaching bill to reduce racial discrimination in history. In 1965, President Johnson signed the Voting Rights Act, which banned discriminatory literacy tests and authorized the federal government to send voting registrars to any district where half or more of the adult population was not registered to vote. This act resulted in a large increase of black voters in several southern states. A third important civil rights act during Johnson's presidency outlawed discrimination in the sale and rental of housing.

Johnson laid before Congress a sweeping legislative program that he hoped would improve the quality of life in the United States and help bring about what he called the Great Society. It concentrated on antipoverty, education, conservation, public works, and urban planning measures, most of which were approved by Congress. Among the major achievements of the Great Society legislation were federal aid to poverty-stricken Appalachia, huge federal appropriations for every level of education (ranging from Head Start for preschoolers through tuition scholarships, loans, and part-time jobs for college students), low-cost public housing, and the first significant environmental acts designed to provide clean air and water. The economic and social measures passed by Congress during the Johnson presidency were much more extensive and more expensive to taxpayers than the domestic program John Kennedy had proposed.

The most important difference between the Kennedy and Johnson administrations was in the conduct of foreign affairs—primarily in the role that the United States played in the Vietnam War. While Kennedy was president, there were about sixteen thousand military advisers in Vietnam, limited to noncombat duties. Johnson escalated U.S. involvement in the conflict enormously until half a million Americans were fighting in Vietnam. In JFK's last two years in the White House, fewer than sixty U.S. advisers were killed in the war. After his assassination, more than fifty-seven thousand Americans gave their lives in the first war that the United States ever lost. (It was also the longest war in American history, not ending until 1973, during the presidential administration of Richard Nixon.)

At home, the war gave rise to angry discord and bloody demonstrations. Antiwar protesters cried out against the tragic conflict on college campuses and street corners throughout the country, in front of the nation's Capitol, and in the halls of Congress as a growing number of lawmakers raised their voices against continuing American participation in the Asian war.

The question often has been raised whether Kennedy would have pulled American forces out of Vietnam had he lived longer and served as president during the time when the tide of the war began turning sharply in favor of the Vietnamese Communists. No one can answer that question. Kennedy might have decided, as Johnson did, to commit large numbers of American warriors in a mighty but desperate effort to prevent the conquest of this non-Communist country in Southeast Asia.

On the other hand, there is evidence that Kennedy might have followed a different course from the one taken by Johnson regarding the escalation of American forces in Vietnam. Less than three months before his death, Kennedy told the news commentator Walter Cronkite that the outcome of the war depended on the South Vietnamese themselves. "It is their war," he said. "We can help them, we can send them equipment, we can send our men out there as advisers . . . but in the final analysis it is their people and their government who have to win or lose this struggle."[14] And, only eight days before he died, JFK announced that the first thousand American advisers in South Vietnam would be on their way home before Christmas. Some of Kennedy's closest aides believed that the president was waiting until he was reelected in 1964 to take the controversial step of ordering all Americans to leave Vietnam.[15]

Death prevented Kennedy from having the opportunity either to end or to escalate the participation of the United States in the Vietnam War, just as death prevented Abraham Lincoln from either accepting or opposing Congress's program for reconstructing the South after the Civil War.

Historians have not considered Kennedy a great president, with achievements that would rank him alongside Lincoln and George Washington. But he did demonstrate wisdom, firmness, and courage, as shown by his restraint in the Bay of Pigs episode, his resolve in the Cuban missile crisis, and his initiative in securing a nuclear test-ban treaty. His presidency lasted only 1,037 days, but it left an indelible record—more perhaps in the way of inspiration than of actual accomplishments. Kennedy brought to the public he served a buoyant, upbeat attitude, a fervent belief that all things are possible—from ending racial discrimination to reaching the moon—and a profound sense of great pride in being American.

JFK's favorite Broadway musical was *Camelot*. The lines he liked best are at the end, when King Arthur knights a youth on the eve of the king's last battle and then tells him:

> Don't let it be forgot
> That once there was a spot
> For one brief shining moment
> That was known as
> Camelot.[16]

MARTIN LUTHER KING, JR.

Martyred Crusader for Civil Rights

In the 1930s, when Martin Luther King, Jr., was growing up in Atlanta, Georgia, black people in the South had to endure severe racial discrimination. Denied access to most of the higher-paying jobs, African-Americans usually had to do menial work for low wages. Many poor black families lived in rundown shacks or shabby, crowded apartments, with barely enough food to survive. Educational opportunities were limited, and young black people had to attend segregated schools and colleges. Even their churches were separate from those attended by whites. For many decades—since the end of Reconstruction in the 1870s—few southern blacks were able to vote.

According to local and state laws throughout the South, African-Americans and whites rode on different railway cars, and railroad stations had black waiting rooms and white waiting rooms, black restrooms and white restrooms, even black drinking fountains and white drinking fountains. Public buses also were segregated: black people had to sit in a special section in the back, and if the white section was full, they had to stand and give their seats to whites. Restaurants and lunch counters, hotels and motels—except in the black sections of towns—refused to serve blacks. Theaters and ballparks sold blacks only their poorest seats, and most public swimming pools, playgrounds, and tennis courts were open only to whites.

Martin Luther King, Jr., was born into this world of prejudice on January 15, 1929. He was the second oldest child of a schoolteacher, Alberta Williams King, and a Baptist preacher, Martin Luther King, Sr., who was commonly called "Daddy King." When Martin, Jr., was still a young child, his father became the senior pastor of the Ebenezer Baptist Church, one of the largest and most influential black churches in Atlanta. The Kings lived in a comfortable, two-story frame house in an all-black, middle-class area. Most of their neighbors were successful lawyers, doctors, teachers, and businessmen and businesswomen.

Daddy King had struggled hard to overcome a poverty-stricken childhood. Born one of ten children to poor share-croppers on a cotton plantation, he doggedly worked his own way through high school and Morehouse College, one of the South's well-known black institutions for higher learning. He achieved success as a minister, and he also set an example of resistance to segregation that strongly impressed young Martin. He served on the executive committee of the local chapter of the National Association for the Advancement of Colored People (NAACP), refused to ride segregated buses, and helped fight for equal pay for black teachers. Daddy King passed the very difficult Georgia literacy test that was given only to blacks as a means of preventing them from voting. Enraged by the barriers to voting rights for blacks, he led a protest march to Atlanta's city hall in 1936, but it failed to bring about any changes that would have permitted more African-Americans to cast their ballots.

Young Martin was bright and earned high grades in

school. He did so well at his studies that he skipped the ninth and twelfth grades and entered Morehouse College at the age of fifteen. At first he was uncertain about what career to pursue, and he considered the possibility of becoming a lawyer. But his chief interest was helping other people, especially the mistreated blacks, and Martin came to believe that he could touch more lives by serving in the pulpit than in the courtroom. So, after graduating from Morehouse, he earned a divinity degree at Crozer Theological Seminary in Chester, Pennsylvania. Martin then attended graduate school at Boston University, where he received a doctorate degree in theology.

While in Boston, King met Coretta Scott of Marion, Alabama, a talented singer, who was studying at the New England Conservatory of Music. They were married in 1953. The Kings had four children—Yolanda, Dexter, Martin, and Bernice.

One event during the time he spent at Crozer was to influence King's future course of action more significantly than perhaps any other single incident in his years as a theology student. In 1949, he heard a stirring lecture about Mahatma Gandhi, delivered by a college president who had just returned from India. "His message," King later wrote, "was so profound and electrifying that I left the meeting and bought a half-dozen books on Gandhi's life and works."[1]

King studied carefully the methods used by Gandhi to mobilize the masses of poor Indians to stand up to the British with their superior weapons and wealth. Gandhi had marshaled the powerful forces of nonviolent resistance and brotherly love to accomplish his goals. Gradually the young black divinity student became convinced that these same forces could be employed to help the oppressed people in the United States.

In 1954, at the age of twenty-five, King became pastor of the Dexter Avenue Baptist Church in Montgomery, Alabama. The youthful minister's sermons, delivered in a rich, melodious voice, inspired, uplifted, and comforted the large congregation. Often he talked about relevant social issues and the power that black churches could wield in the ongoing struggle against segregation and injustice.

In that same year, the Supreme Court handed down a momentous decision in the case of *Brown* v *Board of Education of Topeka*. Speaking for the unanimous court, Chief Justice Earl Warren declared, "We conclude that in the field of public education, the doctrine of 'separate but equal' [schools] has no place. Separate educational facilities are inherently unequal."[2] The Supreme Court thus ruled that separate schools did not provide an equal education for black students and that public schools must therefore be integrated. At first some states and local communities tried to resist enforcement of this court ruling, but in time this landmark decision led to the integration of public schools throughout the country.

The first involvement of Martin Luther King, Jr., in a major campaign to extend civil rights began in December 1955, with an all-out effort to end bus segregation in Montgomery. This crusade stemmed from what had happened to Rosa Parks, a black seamstress, when she took a bus home after work. She paid her bus fare and then sat down in a row located between the "whites only" section in the front and the section for blacks in the rear. African-Americans were permitted to sit in this middle section if the back was filled, but if white persons later boarded the bus, blacks had to stand up and give them their seats. When a white man got on the crowded bus a few stops later, the bus driver ordered Parks to relinquish her seat. She refused to get up, and police arrested her for violating the local bus segregation law.

Parks later explained why she defied the law. "The time had just come when I had been pushed as far as I could stand to be pushed," she said. "I had decided that I would have to know once and for all what rights I had as a human being and a citizen."[3] Besides, she was tired after a long day of work, and her feet hurt.

King and the Reverend Ralph Abernathy of Montgomery's First Baptist Church helped contact other local ministers and black civic leaders, inviting them to a meeting to protest the treatment of Rosa Parks. About fifty people attended, and they agreed to arrange a one-day bus boycott on Monday, December 5, the day that Parks was ordered to appear in court. The ministers promised to urge their congregations not to use the buses that day. Since more than two-thirds of the city's bus riders were black, they hoped this action would have a strong impact.

King was not at all certain whether the boycott would be effective, so on December 5 he and Coretta got up at six o'clock to watch through their window the first bus of the day. It passed by their house without any passengers. The second bus also was empty. The third bus had a few riders, but they were white. The boycott appeared to be succeeding!

Climbing into his car, King drove through various parts of the city and looked into the passing buses. Hardly any blacks could be found aboard. Instead, he saw them sharing rides, hitchhiking, bicycling, using taxis from black taxicab companies that agreed to charge the same fares as the buses did, and walking—sometimes as far as ten or twelve miles.

That morning Rosa Parks was found guilty of disobeying the Montgomery segregation law and fined fourteen dollars. But this was only the beginning of her legal battle. Her case would be appealed to higher courts until finally it would be decided by the Supreme Court of the United States.

That afternoon black leaders in Montgomery met to form an official organization for their protest and determine whether to extend the bus boycott. They set up the Montgomery Improvement Association (MIA) and elected King its president. Then they decided to continue the boycott until bus segregation in their city ended.

The same evening King addressed a mass meeting at his church. Amid cheers and loud applause from the huge throng that packed the building and overflowed onto the grounds outside, King reassured his listeners that their cause was just. He then cautioned them not to resort to any acts of violence as they defied segregation. "If we protest courageously, and yet with Christian love," King concluded, "when the history books are written in the future, somebody will have to say, 'There lived a race of people, of black people, of people who had the moral courage to stand up for their rights. And thereby they injected a new meaning into the veins of history and civilization.' "4

At first officials of the bus company made no serious effort to reach an agreement with the black leaders. They were convinced that the protest would end when the first rainy days and cold weather arrived. But the rain and cold weather did not stop the blacks from boycotting the buses. The bus company officers and the city commissioners then met with the MIA executive board, but the only concession they were willing to make was to ask the bus drivers to be more polite to black patrons.

As the boycott dragged on, members of the segregationist White Citizens Council spearheaded a campaign to force the blacks to give in. They tried to make the black taxicab companies raise their fares. They threatened car-pool drivers with loss of insurance and licenses. They ordered police to give tickets to these drivers for blocking traffic and to riders waiting on street corners for being vagrants. King himself was arrested and taken to jail, allegedly for driving thirty miles per hour in a twenty-five-mile-per-hour zone.

When Ralph Abernathy learned that King was being held, he hurried to the jail and asked to bail out his friend. The officer in charge replied that bail could not be posted until the next morning. Meanwhile, a large number of African-Americans began assembling outside the jail. They crowded onto the steps of the building, along the sidewalk, and even far out into the street. The police officer who had denied King immediate bail became nervous when he saw the huge group of blacks outside. He hastily fingerprinted and photographed the civil rights leader and then sneered, "All right, King. You're being released. . . . Now get out."[5]

From the first days of the boycott, the Kings had been receiving threatening and obscene phone calls and letters. By mid-January, they were getting about forty hate letters a day, which King took the time to answer. On January 30, while he was speaking to a mass rally, King's home was bombed. Coretta King was inside with their baby daughter, Yolanda, and a woman friend. Hearing a deafening explosion on the front porch, Mrs. King grabbed Yolanda, and the women rushed to the back of the house. King hurried home and was greatly relieved when he found his family had not been injured.

Word of the bombing spread quickly through the African-American community, and many angered blacks, some armed with guns, rushed to King's home. The white policemen at the scene of the crime were soon outnumbered by the irate, armed blacks, who refused to disperse. A bloody racial clash seemed inevitable. Then King stepped outside and addressed his followers. "If you have weapons, take them home; if you do not have them, please do not seek to get them," he begged the crowd. "We cannot solve this problem through retaliatory violence. We must meet violence with nonviolence."[6]

The segregationists tried other tactics to end the bus boycott. In February 1956, King and about one hundred other blacks were charged with breaking an old state law against boycotting. King was found guilty, but appeals kept his case in the courts for months. On November 13, the city of Montgomery sought a court order to prohibit the black car pools. As he listened to the proceedings in court, King was discouraged because he knew that the boycott could not continue to be effective without the many car pools organized to take blacks to and from work. But just after the luncheon recess, his despair changed to joy. A reporter handed him a news dispatch saying that on that day the Supreme Court had ruled that the state and local laws of Alabama requiring segregation on buses were unconstitutional and thereby overturned!

Another month passed before the local government of Montgomery enforced this Supreme Court decision. On December 21, 1956—one year and sixteen days after the boycott began—King boarded the first integrated bus. He and a white minister friend shared a seat in the front. The "miracle of Montgomery" finally had come to pass.

The bus boycott made King a national figure and the country's most prominent African-American civil rights leader. *Time* magazine featured him in a cover story, and he wrote a widely read book, *Stride toward Freedom: The Montgomery Story*. In 1957, he met with other black ministers to form an alliance—the Southern Christian Leadership Conference (SCLC)—that would coordinate their efforts to combat segregation throughout the South. The charismatic King was unanimously elected president of the new organization. One of the SCLC's chief goals was to register more black voters in the South. On Lincoln's birthday in 1958, mass rallies to publicize the cause of giving blacks the ballot were held in twenty-one southern cities, but white segregationists continued to find ways to prevent most blacks from voting.

The headquarters of SCLC were in Atlanta, and as its activities increased, King spent much of his time there, working on civil rights projects. In 1959, he decided to move his family to Atlanta and accept the position of co-pastor at his father's large Ebenezer Baptist Church. A short time later, a group of black students in Greensboro, North Carolina, sat down at a segregated lunch counter and declared they would not leave until after they had been served. When their orders were not taken, they stayed at the counter all day. This marked the beginning of the sit-in movement, which quickly spread to more than fifty southern cities.

King was frequently called on to train the sit-in demonstrators. He told them to dress neatly and act politely at all times. No matter how much they were abused or humiliated, they were never to retaliate with violent actions. At some counters they were hit by white thugs who opposed integration. Some protesters were doused with ketchup or mustard, and lighted cigarettes were put into their hair. Still, they refused to give up and leave the counters—or fight back and defy the principle of nonviolence. The sit-in demonstrations gave birth to a permanent and powerful youth organization called the Student Nonviolent Coordinating Committee (SNCC).

Sometimes King personally took part in the sit-in demonstrations. He and other black protesters were arrested and jailed for trespassing when they sat-in at a lunch counter in a large Atlanta department store. Officials from nearby DeKalb County then asked that King be turned over to them so they could try him for being arrested while on probation. (He had been placed on probation after police had stopped his car because he was driving with a white woman activist and the officer noticed that his driver's license had expired.)

King was found guilty, denied bail, and sentenced to four months of hard labor in a prison camp. Coretta, who was then pregnant with her third child, broke down in tears when she heard her husband's harsh sentence for a minor violation stemming from a traffic ticket. Senator John F. Kennedy, who was then the Democratic candidate for the presidency, also heard about the unjust sentence and phoned Mrs. King to assure her he would do whatever he could to help her husband. Three days later, as a result of Kennedy's intervention, King was released on bail. Blacks throughout the country were impressed by the courageous stand Kennedy had taken in behalf of their leader, even though it meant risking the votes of many white southerners. In the close election that fall, Kennedy carried almost three-quarters of the black vote, which helped provide his razor-thin margin of victory.

In the spring of 1961, King met with the new president. He found that Kennedy was sympathetic toward the needs of blacks, but at that time he was not prepared to put a strong civil rights bill before Congress. The president explained that such a bill would not pass because of the southerners' power in Congress; it also would anger southern Democrats to the extent that they might then vote against other parts of his legislative program. Kennedy argued that his economic and social measures favoring minimum-wage increases, low-cost housing, and federal aid to education would benefit blacks even more than whites. He promised King that he would use his executive powers to advance the cause of civil rights.[7]

Early in May 1961, the Congress of Racial Equality (CORE), under the leadership of James Farmer, decided to take the sit-in demonstrations on the road. CORE was determined to test recent Supreme Court rulings that banned segregation on interstate buses and trains and in their terminals. Thirteen civil rights activists, including six whites, boarded two buses in Washington, D.C., and headed south. Called freedom riders, they planned to cross every state in the Deep South and stop in many cities and towns along the way.

At Anniston, Alabama, a screaming mob attacked one of the buses with iron bars, smashed windows, slashed tires, and tossed a fire bomb that started a fire in the bus. Choking and gasping for air, the freedom riders barely escaped before the bus exploded. When they reached the ground, several of them were beaten mercilessly. Nine men were arrested for the assault, but none of them was punished. When the second bus reached Birmingham, the local police stood by while members of the racist Ku Klux Klan hit the freedom riders with bats and iron pipes.

When the freedom riders reached Montgomery, a huge group of angry whites attacked them savagely. King was in Chicago at the time, and, after watching with anguish a televised account of the violent ordeal, he decided to fly immediately to the Alabama capital. The next night he addressed a mass rally in Reverend Abernathy's Montgomery church. Among the audience of black supporters were the freedom riders disguised as members of the choir.

As King spoke, a white crowd outside tossed rocks through the church's stained-glass windows, showering people in the pews with jagged pieces of glass. From the pulpit the civil rights leader cautioned the congregation not to respond to violence with militant action, and more than twelve hundred courageous African-Americans raised their voices in the black freedom anthem, "We Shall Overcome." The rioting mob appeared on the verge of breaking down the church doors when federal marshals, ordered to the scene by Attorney General Robert Kennedy, began arriving to help soldiers from the National Guard disperse the unruly throng with tear gas and clubs. Then the officers escorted the people inside the church to safety.

King believed that Birmingham was the most segregated city in the nation, and in 1963 he launched a major civil rights campaign in that city, which was the industrial center of the South. On April 12, almost a thousand blacks lined the streets as King and Abernathy led about fifty demonstrators toward the Birmingham city hall. They had marched only eight blocks when they were confronted by Police Commissioner Eugene (Bull) Connor, an extreme racist. When the two black preachers walked up to Connor, they knelt in front of him in prayer. Suddenly the police grabbed them by the back of their shirts, threw them into paddy wagons, and then seized the other marchers. King was placed in solitary confinement in a dark cell and was not allowed to talk to his family or a lawyer for more than twenty-four hours.

While he was in jail, King was handed a newspaper letter composed by white Alabama clergymen who condemned his activist tactics for disturbing the atmosphere of peace and calm in Birmingham. Soon the black leader was busy writing a forceful reply on scraps of paper and in the margins of the newspaper. "We know through painful experience," King wrote,

> ━━━━━━━━━ *that freedom is never voluntarily given by the oppressor; it must be demanded by the oppressed. . . . If our white brothers dismiss as "rabble rousers" and "outside agitators" those of us who employ nonviolent action and if they refuse to support our nonviolent efforts, millions of Negroes will, out of frustration and despair, seek solace and security in black-nationalist ideologies—a development that would eventually lead to a frightening racial nightmare.*[8]

This eloquent statement, later published as a pamphlet by a Quaker group as *Letter from a Birmingham Jail*, became a classic expression of nonviolent civil disobedience.

Out on bail, King worked with other black leaders to organize a children's crusade for integration. They assumed that the police would not dare to harass innocent youngsters. Early in May 1963, a thousand children marched two abreast into downtown Birmingham, singing freedom songs. More than nine hundred of them were arrested. Even more children marched the next day. When they refused to heed Bull Connor's command to halt, he ordered fire engines to turn their powerful hoses on the young demonstrators. The jets of water hit like hammers. They drove some students against the walls of buildings; others were struck to the ground.

Some of the black spectators who were horrified by the brutal treatment of children were not part of King's nonviolent forces. They began to fight back, pelting the police with bricks, rocks, and bottles. Connor retaliated by unleashing attack dogs on the blacks. Police clubbed many people, and more than 250 African-Americans were arrested.

People throughout the nation watched with astonishment as the cruel events at Birmingham flashed across their TV screens. Demonstrations and riots led by irate blacks erupted in many cities. President Kennedy knew that he could no longer avoid a clash with southern lawmakers by withholding support for meaningful civil rights legislation. In June 1963, he laid before Congress the most sweeping civil rights bill in history (see Chapter 5). But southern legislators blocked its passage while Kennedy lived, and it was not enacted until 1964, when President Lyndon Johnson pushed it through Congress.

To help convince lawmakers to vote for President Kennedy's civil rights bill and to dramatize the growing strength of the nonviolent protest against racial segregation, black leaders planned a mass march and rally in front of the Lincoln Memorial in Washington, D.C. They encouraged black and white clergy throughout the country to take part in the march with their congregations. A crowd of about one hundred thousand was expected. Government officials, including the president, were fearful that such a huge throng of people moving through the nation's capital might set off ugly clashes with unsympathetic bystanders. Acts of violence could enflame the already tense relations between the races and reduce the chances of Congress's passing the civil rights bill.

The demonstration occurred as planned, on August 28, 1963, but estimates of the number of marchers were much too low. The size of the crowd swelled to more than 250,000. The march on Washington proved to be the largest single civil rights demonstration in the nation's history—and was entirely peaceful, without any scuffles throughout the day. Many blacks and whites clasped hands as they gathered for the program. Millions more would see the events at home or at work on television.

Folksingers led the crowd in freedom songs and black spirituals. Many speakers stepped to the microphone to stress the importance of the civil rights cause. The listeners cheered enthusiastically as the last speaker was introduced—Martin Luther King, Jr. The "I Have a Dream" speech that King delivered that hot afternoon in Washington, D.C., stirred the hearts and consciences of Americans as no message had since Lincoln's Gettysburg Address.

In his deep baritone voice, King fervently proclaimed:

> ▬▬▬▬▬ *I have a dream that one day on the red hills of Georgia the sons of former slaves and the sons of former slave owners will be able to sit down together at the table of brotherhood. . . . I have a dream that my four little children will one day live in a nation where they will not be judged by the color of their skin, but the content of their character. . . . When we let it [freedom] ring from every village and every hamlet, from every state and every city, we will be able to speed up the day when all God's children, black men and white men, Jews and Gentiles, Protestants and Catholics, will be able to join hands and sing in the words of the old Negro spiritual, "Free at last! Free at last! Thank God Almighty, we are free at last!"* [9]

In 1964, King was awarded the Nobel Peace Prize, an international honor of enormous prestige that is given annually to the person or organization who has contributed most to the promotion of world peace. King was the third black and the twelfth American ever to win this award, which was established by Alfred Nobel in 1895. He donated all the prize money—fifty-four thousand dollars—to the civil rights movement.

Even at the time he was hailed as a champion of world peace, King was deeply troubled by various outbreaks of racial conflict. In the same year that he received the Nobel Prize, there had been severe rioting in Brooklyn, Chicago, and Philadelphia. Three civil rights workers had been murdered in Mississippi. King was also concerned by the growing number of blacks who were becoming militant and denouncing his nonviolent philosophy. Black Power, they demanded, now and forever! They wanted to lash back with force at the whites who had kept them oppressed generation after generation and continued to treat them as second-class citizens. Many years of bitter frustration and deep-seated despair had sapped their patience, and they cried out for weapons and warfare. King clearly understood their feelings, but he argued against the course of action they demanded. He felt that blacks, constituting only 12 percent of the population, could never win in any violent confrontation and that the nonviolent protest movement stood the only chance of providing permanent success.

The Civil Rights Act of 1964 had desegregated public accommodations, such as restaurants, hotels, and theaters. But the battle against prejudice had only begun. Martin Luther King, Jr., was one of the leaders who believed that the key to securing more civil rights for blacks was to give them the ballot. If African-Americans voted in substantial numbers, racists could be driven from office and segregationist laws could be overturned. Early in 1965, the Southern Christian Leadership Conference campaigned to register black voters in Alabama. It initially focused attention on the town of Selma, about fifty miles west of Montgomery. Selma was an ideal target for dramatizing the lack of black power at the polls. Its 15,000 blacks outnumbered the town's whites, yet only about 350 blacks were registered to vote.

In January 1965, many African-Americans tried to register to vote in Selma. At the courthouse they stood in line for hours waiting to register, only to be told that the office was closed that day. Now and then they were allowed to fill out forms, but usually these were thrown out because of some minor technicality, such as failing to dot an *i* or not putting a period after a middle initial.

To protest the problems encountered by blacks in trying to register to vote, King and Abernathy led a mass march of about 265 demonstrators to the courthouse. All of them were arrested for parading without a permit and thrown into jail. From his jail cell, King continued to lead the campaign, and every day more black protesters were arrested. Soon there were about three thousand blacks in jail—more than the number of blacks on Selma's voting rolls.

For five days King remained in jail. After he was released on bail, he went to Washington, D.C., to talk with President Lyndon Johnson about the troubles the blacks faced in their voter registration campaign. While King was away from Selma, a group of student demonstrators were chased out of town by the sheriff and his deputies, who used electric cattle prods to keep them running.

When King returned, he planned a march from Selma to the state capital at Montgomery, where the civil rights advocates intended to confront George Wallace, the racist governor of Alabama. Wallace announced that the march was illegal, but more than five hundred brave men and women set off on the fifty-four-mile pilgrimage. After traveling about six blocks, they crossed the Pettus Bridge; on the other side of the bridge they saw a wall of state troopers standing shoulder to shoulder. As the marchers tried to proceed, the troopers attacked them with bull whips, rubber hoses wrapped with barbed wire, nightsticks, and tear gas. Helpless against this vicious onslaught, the unarmed marchers were forced to retreat. Many were injured; some required hospitalization. The blacks had lost the battle, but they were determined not to surrender their cause.

King called for another march to Montgomery and asked religious leaders all over the country to join the crusade. Soon more than four hundred ministers, rabbis, priests, and nuns arrived in Selma. The SCLC had sought to convince a federal judge to overrule Governor Wallace's ban on the march, but on March 8, 1965—the day before the march was to begin—the judge issued a temporary order forbidding the event. To avoid breaking the law, King then decided to compromise, angering black militants, who accused the Nobel Prize winner of being too soft and lenient to be an effective leader. King and about fifteen hundred marchers, including the many volunteers from various religious faiths, proceeded as far as the Pettus Bridge, where they were met by state troopers. Then the group knelt down to pray and returned to the church where the march had originated.

The brief demonstration had been peaceful, no one was hurt, and King intended to wait for a further hearing from the court. That evening, however, the peace was shattered. Three white Unitarian ministers who had been among the marchers were savagely beaten by members of the Ku Klux Klan. One of them, James Reeb from Boston, suffered a crushed skull and died two days later.

Outraged by Reeb's murder, President Johnson solemnly addressed a joint session of Congress and demanded legislation that would give blacks in the South the same voting rights that whites had long enjoyed. ". . . What happened in Selma," the president declared, "is part of a far larger movement which reaches into every section and every state of America. It is the effort of American Negroes to secure for themselves the full blessings of American life. Their cause must be our cause, too. Because it is not just Negroes, but really it is all of us who must overcome the crippling legacy of bigotry and injustice." Then President Johnson concluded, "And we shall overcome!"[10]

A federal court finally approved the march to Montgomery, and the five-day trek from Selma began on March 21. At the head of about three thousand marchers strode King, Abernathy, Ralph Bunche, the black American who held a high position in the United Nations, and Rabbi Abraham Heschel of the Jewish Theological Seminary of America. When they reached Montgomery, their ranks were joined by nearly twenty-five thousand civil rights activists from many parts of the nation. This huge army of committed pilgrims marched peacefully and triumphantly to the steps of the Alabama state capitol. Even though Governor Wallace refused to speak to them, the demonstra-

tors knew that their successful march—after repeated dis-
couraging setbacks—had advanced the cause that they
championed. Moreover, on August 6, 1965, President
Johnson signed the Voting Rights Act, which removed
most of the barriers that had prevented southern blacks
from voting (see Chapter 5).

Just a few days after this historic act became law, the
Watts section of Los Angeles, peopled almost entirely by
blacks, burst into violence. Black militants battled police
and ten thousand National Guard troops were hastily sent
into the area. Scores of buildings were set afire; countless
stores were looted; millions of dollars' worth of property was
destroyed or badly damaged. In one of the most devastating
riots in the nation's history, more than thirty-five hundred
people were arrested and thirty-five blacks were killed.

King flew to Los Angeles to inspect the damage and
counsel the blacks in Watts not to resort to any more violence. He talked to many of the local victims and learned
that abject poverty was the principal cause of the rioting.
Large numbers of blacks, many of them unemployed, had
endured wretched living conditions for a long time. Finally,
the lid blew off, and they expressed their anger and despair
in street warfare. In Watts and in many other cities, blacks
were turning in increasing numbers to the ideas that King
had opposed—to bloody riots rather than nonviolence and
peaceful demonstrations, to separation from whites rather
than integration.

The time had come, King decided, to concentrate more
of his time and attention on the problem of poverty as it
affected blacks both in the North and in the South. In
February 1966, he and his family moved into a tenement
apartment in Chicago, where he was one of the leaders in
developing the Chicago Project. Its major objectives were
to help African-Americans secure better jobs, decent housing that was both affordable and integrated, and school
desegregation. On July 10, designated as "Freedom Sunday," King addressed a giant rally at Chicago's Soldier's

Field, telling the huge crowd that the conditions that caused black slums must be eliminated. A few days later, rioting erupted in Chicago, and before it ended, two blacks had died and hundreds of people had been injured.

In the mid-1960s, American participation in the Vietnam War was growing at a rapid rate. King felt that the proportion of blacks serving and dying in the war was much too high, and that the billions of dollars needed by the federal government to fight in Asia could better be spent on projects to help poor people in the United States. In 1967, at Riverside Church in New York City, King delivered a major address against continuing the American role in the war. He knew that this message would anger President Johnson, who had been sympathetic to the cause of equality and justice for African-Americans, but the Baptist preacher put the needs of poor people above his friendship with the president.

King wanted to dramatize the plight of the poor with a Poor People's March on Washington that would include not only blacks but also representatives of other poverty-stricken groups, such as Hispanics, Native Americans, and whites who had few financial resources. While he was organizing this march, King was asked to take part in a demonstration in Memphis for local sanitation workers, who were mainly blacks. They had gone on strike because the city officials had ignored their demands for higher pay and better working conditions.

Helping the sanitation workers in Memphis fit in with King's overall plan to aid poor people, so he agreed to lead their march. But when the protesters had advanced less than three blocks, King heard the sound of shattering glass. He soon discovered that some black militants were mixed in among the peaceful marchers. They started throwing rocks at windows, breaking into stores, and looting. King and his followers dropped out of the march, but the militants refused to disperse. They clashed with police, and their rioting continued until one black had been killed and sixty others were clubbed and injured.

King was shocked and saddened by what had happened, but he was determined to prove that the blacks in Memphis could conduct an orderly march that would not be marred by any fighting. So he decided to lead a second march for the sanitation workers on April 8. King arrived in Memphis a few days before the demonstration to make careful preparations. On April 4, he spent most of the day closeted with his chief aides in a second-floor room at the Lorraine Motel. Shortly before the black leaders were to go to dinner, King stepped outside to the balcony, leaned over the railing, and chatted with friends in the parking lot below.

Suddenly, the loud thud of a rifle shot was heard. A bullet tore through King's face and neck, and he staggered backward, falling onto the balcony floor. He was rushed to a hospital, but his wound proved fatal. The greatest prophet of nonviolence since Gandhi had died, like Gandhi, from an assassin's bullet.

The tragic irony of King's life was that the end of it set off the worst outburst of rioting, arson, and looting in the nation's history. A curfew was declared that evening in Memphis, but it did not prevent a wild night of street warfare. By midnight, eighty people had been jailed and National Guard troops ringed the city. Similar disturbances broke out in 168 cities and towns. None was hit worse than Washington, D.C., where an incredible 711 fires were started. Buildings only a few blocks from the White House were set to the torch. President Johnson ordered flags flown at half-mast on all federal buildings and asked the nation to honor King's memory by ending the violence, but the terror continued for several days and nights. Nationwide, the rioting took thirty-nine lives, and 21,270 people were injured. To restore order, 55,000 soldiers were required.[11]

An intensive search was started for King's assassin. Apparently the killer had aimed the fatal bullet from the second-floor window of a bathroom in a rooming house that adjoined the Lorraine Motel's parking lot. After the shot had been fired, other tenants of the rooming house saw a white man with a rifle running down the hall. When he reached the street, he was carrying the murder weapon wrapped in a bedspread and an overnight bag filled with personal articles, such as underwear, soap, and shoe polish. All of a sudden, a police car appeared and frightened the assassin, and he got rid of the things he was carrying by tossing them in the doorway of a nearby store. Then he sped away in a white Mustang.

Fingerprints on the articles he had discarded identified the murderer as James Earl Ray. He was an escaped convict from the Missouri state penitentiary, who had a long record of crimes involving armed robbery, car thefts, and forgery. After King's murder, Ray eluded the police and FBI agents for two months, by escaping to Canada and then to Europe. He was finally captured in London on June 8, 1968, as he tried to board a plane bound for Belgium.

When he appeared in court in Memphis, Ray pleaded guilty and was sentenced to a term of ninety-nine years in prison. Why he committed the crime and whether he had any conspirators are two questions that have never been fully answered. People who knew Ray described him as a racist, but it could not be proved that his antiblack feelings were intense enough to cause him to murder King. Perhaps he was hired by some individual or organization and promised a large sum of money for ending the life of the civil rights leader. James W. Clarke, an authority on political assassinations, wrote in 1982 that the case against Ray was overwhelming, but it was unlikely that he acted alone. Clarke concluded that Ray was part of a conspiracy that had made a deal with wealthy, hate-mongering segregationists to receive a payment of fifty thousand dollars for silencing forever the voice of a great apostle of brotherly love.[12]

King left an indelible impact on the civil rights movement. In many areas, from riding buses to removing barriers that prevented voting, he played a major role in helping blacks attain equality and justice. A grateful nation acknowledged the lasting contributions of this peaceful warrior in various ways. Countless streets, parks, playgrounds, and schools were named for him. In 1983, Congress established a federal holiday honoring King. The day is celebrated on the third Monday in January.

Today, more than two decades after King's death, the noble crusade that he helped lead throughout his adult life has not yet achieved all its goals. Many blacks and other minorities still have low-paying jobs, shortages of food, inadequate housing, and limited opportunities to acquire a good education. Their numbers include comparatively few doctors, lawyers, and other professionals. Many are forced by poverty to live in ghettos where crime and drugs are prevalent. Until their basic needs are satisfied, many millions of people cannot enjoy or participate in the American dream.

CHAPTER SEVEN

ROBERT F. KENNEDY

Murdered Opponent of the Vietnam War

"I was the seventh of nine children," Robert Francis (Bobby) Kennedy once said, "and when you come from that far down you have to struggle to survive." Bobby was ten years younger than his brother Joe, Jr., and eight years younger than brother John (Jack). But from early childhood, he tried to keep up with the older Kennedy boys in every kind of sport. When he was only four years old, he would jump off the family sailboat, determined to swim with his brothers, who had to rescue the little boy after each attempt. "It showed either a lot of guts," said Jack, "or no sense at all."[1]

The fierce drive to compete was instilled in the Kennedy children by their domineering, hard-driving father. Joseph Kennedy, Sr., was not satisfied just to have his youngsters take part in swimming meets, tennis matches, sailing races, and football games. Winning was what mattered most to the head of the Kennedy family. "Coming in second is no good," he told his children. "The important thing is to win!

Don't come in second or third—that doesn't count, but win, win, WIN!"[2]

Bobby felt physically inferior to his brothers and considered himself the "runt of the litter." Even in adulthood, he was shorter and smaller than Joe, Jr., Jack, and his younger brother, Edward (Teddy). But the will to live up to his father's expectations that he succeed in competition was deeply etched into Bobby's character. Instead of making excuses for his slight build, Bobby played harder, more enthusiastically, and with less concern about injuring himself than did many other boys who were larger and stronger. These childhood traits of grit and determination helped shape his entire life; in his public career he was often referred to as an aggressive, tireless battler who would leave no stone unturned in the pursuit of his goals.

Bobby was born on November 20, 1925, in Brookline, Massachusetts, a suburb of Boston. A short time later, the Kennedy family moved to New York City and then to the suburb of Bronxville. When Bobby was twelve, his father was appointed ambassador to Great Britain, and the family lived for two years in London. In September 1939, World War II began, and Joseph Kennedy feared that German warplanes soon would start bombing London. So he sent his family back to Bronxville.

Because the Kennedys made so many moves, Bobby attended several elementary and secondary schools. After returning to the United States from England, he was sent to Portsmouth Priory, a Catholic boarding school in Rhode Island. The Kennedy family were devout Catholics, and the two and one-half years that Bobby spent at Portsmouth Priory helped provide a strong foundation for his religious beliefs. In September 1942, he transferred to Milton Academy, near Boston, where he prepared for admission to Harvard University.

Attending college, however, was not uppermost in Bobby's mind at that time. The United States was now involved in World War II, and his brothers Joe, Jr., and

Jack both were serving in the Navy. Bobby wanted to follow in his brothers' footsteps, so, just before his eighteenth birthday, he enlisted in a Navy program for training pilots. It called for a period of college studies, followed by preflight training, and then active duty as a commissioned officer. Bobby was sent to an officer training school at Harvard for eight months, then to Bates College in Lewiston, Maine, for seven months, and back to Harvard for another eight months. On weekends he often relaxed at the spacious, comfortable Kennedy family home at Hyannis Port, Massachusetts.

Joe Kennedy, Jr., was a naval pilot stationed in England; Jack Kennedy was a PT boat commander in the South Pacific. Bobby wanted to play an active role in the war, too, and he grew impatient sitting on the sidelines as he took more and more college courses. His desire for active service increased after Jack became a war hero in August 1943, when his PT boat was sliced in half by a Japanese destroyer and he had to swim five hours to reach land, dragging the boat's injured engineer behind him. And after Joe, Jr., was killed the following year in an aerial mission over the English Channel, Bobby was determined to find some way in which he could help fight America's enemies. But the war ended before he was called to active duty.

Late in 1945, a newly commissioned destroyer named the USS *Joseph P. Kennedy, Jr.*, was ready for sea duty. Bobby wanted to be a sailor on this ship named for his brother. So he dropped out of the program that trained naval pilots, giving up his chance to become an officer, and joined the crew of the *Kennedy* in the lowest rank of seaman apprentice. On its first cruise, the *Kennedy* sailed in the Caribbean Sea, and for four months Bobby scrubbed its decks and did other menial chores. Disappointed because nothing exciting happened on the long voyage, he returned home, and soon afterward his service in the Navy ended.

This was the summer of 1946, an important time for the Kennedy family. Jack was running for a seat in the

House of Representatives from a district mainly in East Boston. Bobby rolled up his sleeves and started working for his brother's election. He took part in strategy sessions, hanged posters, handed out leaflets, manned telephones, and walked mile after mile to tell all the voters whose hands he shook why they should send his brother to Congress. Jack won the Democratic nomination and then the fall election against his Republican opponent. Bobby had never before participated so actively in an election campaign. Even though the experience was tiring, he found it exhilarating, and it provided excellent training for the many elections in which he was later involved.

That same year Bobby returned to Harvard and majored in government. His chief interest, however, was playing football, and he tried out for the position of end on the college team. Driven by an obsessive desire to play well and become a letterman, every day he arrived early at the practice field and stayed late. Bobby weighed only 155 pounds and was not a fast runner; time and time again he would catch a pass and then be slammed to the turf by faster, heavier players.

In his senior year, Bobby finally started his first game at right end and, after catching a pass, scored the only touchdown of his college career. A few days later, he broke his leg in practice but told no one and kept on trying to play until he collapsed on the field. The injury ended his chance to play on the starting team, but he still hoped that he could win his letter. There was a Harvard tradition that any player who took part in the game against Yale at the end of the season would be awarded the coveted letter.

Bobby's leg still had not entirely healed and was heavily bandaged when Harvard played Yale. He sat on the bench feeling dejected, both because Harvard was losing and because he was not playing in his final game. Suddenly, in the closing minutes of the contest, young Kennedy heard his number called by a sympathetic coach. Joyfully he hobbled onto the field and took part in a few plays, thus enabling him to win his letter. He regarded this as an important achievement, especially since neither of his older brothers had lettered in football while they were at Harvard.

After graduating from college, Bobby enrolled at the University of Virginia Law School. He began dating Ethel Skakel, the daughter of a prominent Chicago businessman and the sixth of seven children. Like Bobby, Ethel enjoyed outdoor sports. She liked to ride horses, swim, play tennis, and take an active part in the touch football games that became a trademark of the Kennedy clan. She considered it a great compliment when John Kennedy once said that as a football player, "Ethel's very good. You ought to see her run and pass."[3] Unlike Bobby, who tended to be shy and often moody, Ethel had a warm, vivacious personality.

Bobby and Ethel were married on June 19, 1950, while he was still in law school. In time, they acquired a large, rambling estate in Virginia called Hickory Hill, which was an ideal place for their eleven children. Hickory Hill had a swimming pool, tennis courts, and stables for horses and ponies. The Kennedy children had a variety of other animals, including several dogs, a cat, a donkey, chickens, roosters, ducks, and, for a while, even a seal.

When Bobby earned his law degree in 1951, his prosperous father offered to set up a law practice for him in any city that he chose. Bobby, however, was not interested in establishing a private law practice, so he went to work as an investigator for the Department of Justice. His first assignment was to present before a Brooklyn grand jury a case against two former government officials in the Truman administration who were charged with corruption. Young Kennedy unearthed enough evidence to help convict one of the officials of evading $100,000 in income taxes and the other of illegally interfering in a tax lawsuit.

Bobby soon discovered that a difficult and lengthy process had to be undertaken to bring most criminals to justice. "There's quite a spread between indictment [making formal charges] and conviction," he said. "It's one thing to accuse a man; it's another to convince a jury of his guilt."[4] Still, he found the work not only challenging but fascinating. Soon, however, family obligation summoned him back to Massachusetts. Congressman Jack Kennedy had decided to run for the Senate, and his brother's services were needed in the campaign. Bobby left his job to give his brother Jack a helping hand.

It was during this 1952 campaign that Bobby acquired the reputation of being ruthless and ill-tempered. One day a powerful labor leader sat chatting in the Kennedy headquarters. Bobby, who toiled day and night for his brother's election, could not tolerate a campaign helper who sat idly by when there was so much to do. He ushered the labor leader out of the office and told him angrily, "If you're not going to work, don't hang around here."[5] Another time he threw a politician out of the headquarters for swearing in the presence of women. He confronted the Democratic governor of Massachusetts at the State House and fiercely accused him of making a speech that hurt his brother's campaign. Livid with rage, the governor telephoned Joseph Kennedy and demanded that he "keep that fresh kid of yours out of my sight from now on."[6]

Jack won the election (see Chapter 5), and in 1953 Bobby became an assistant counsel to the Senate Permanent Subcommittee on Investigations. The United States was then fighting the Korean War, and the subcommittee directed Bobby to find out how many ships from non-Communist countries continued to trade with Red China during the war. He learned that in 1952 and 1953 at least 355 vessels owned by nineteen shipping firms of non-Communist nations had been sending cargoes to the Communists, and that two British-owned ships had transported Chinese Communist troops along the coast of China. The war was drawing to a close by the time Bobby's report was made public, but its startling discoveries were revealed in newspaper articles throughout the country.[7]

From 1954 to 1960, Kennedy worked for the Senate

Select Committee on Improper Activities in the Labor and Management Field, and in 1957 he became chief counsel for this committee. In this position he investigated labor racketeering and learned that some powerful labor leaders were diverting funds from union treasuries for their own use. He unearthed damaging evidence against Dave Beck, president of the International Brotherhood of Teamsters Union, and his successor, Jimmy Hoffa. After lengthy trials, both of these men eventually were convicted and sentenced to prison.

This investigation of labor bosses, some of whom had links to gangsters in the underworld, made newspaper headlines and brought Robert Kennedy national prominence. In 1955, the Junior Chamber of Commerce named him one of the ten outstanding young men of that year. Bobby's fame increased when he wrote a widely read book on corruption and crime titled *The Enemy Within*, which was published in 1960. Later, he wrote three other books: *Just Friends and Brave Enemies* (1962), *Pursuit of Justice* (1964), and *Thirteen Days: A Memoir of the Cuban Missile Crisis* (1969).

Bobby set aside his own successful career as a government investigator to manage the 1960 presidential campaign of his brother Jack. With enormous drive and almost ceaseless energy, he crisscrossed the entire country, trying to convince voters in primary elections and delegates to the Democratic convention that Jack was the best candidate for the party's nomination. His tactics were aggressive, and his manner was often brusque and stern, but he played a large part in securing the presidential nomination for his older brother.

Jack then asked Senator Lyndon B. Johnson of Texas to be his running mate. At first Bobby was strongly opposed to the selection of Johnson as the vice presidential candidate because he feared that a white southerner on the national ticket would antagonize blacks and northern liberal voters. Johnson helped the Democratic nominees win some badly needed states in the South, so his value to the ticket in this extremely close election outweighed any disadvantages (see Chapter 5). But Bobby's criticism of Johnson angered the Texan, and in the years that followed these two outspoken Democrats resented each other.

When President-elect Kennedy began choosing his cabinet members, he asked Bobby to be his attorney general. Bobby shook his head no and a frown wrinkled his forehead. He reminded his older brother that naming a Kennedy to his cabinet would cause many people to charge JFK with nepotism (showing favoritism to a relative in the distribution of political offices). Moreover, Bobby, who was then only thirty-five, felt he was too young to hold such an important government office. "I need you," JFK insisted. "I need someone I can trust, someone with whom I can talk things over frankly."

Bobby protested that he did not have enough legal experience for the job, but Jack assured him that he could do the work and that he should "never be afraid to express an honest opinion on any subject."[8] The newly elected president finally persuaded his brother to take the position. During the Kennedy administration, Bobby became JFK's chief adviser on civil rights and also a leading counselor on foreign affairs, national security, and domestic policy.

As head of the Department of Justice and the highest law officer in the national government, Attorney General Kennedy had to protect the rights of all citizens and see that the country's laws were obeyed. When he took office in 1961, securing the civil rights of blacks, especially in the South, was a major domestic issue, and in this area the youthful attorney general made his most significant and lasting contributions.

In May 1961, when the freedom riders were being assaulted in southern cities for trying to integrate buses and terminals, the attorney general took bold steps to help protect the civil rights advocates. Learning that the freedom riders were being brutally attacked in Montgomery, Alabama, Kennedy sent nearly seven hundred federal marshals to that troubled city. He also instructed the governor of Alabama, John Patterson, to dispatch National Guardsmen to the Montgomery church where Dr. Martin Luther King, Jr., was addressing a huge rally. An angry mob of white segregationists had gathered outside the church and was threatening King and his audience, which was composed of local African-Americans and the freedom riders who had sought protection in the church.

Governor Patterson felt the freedom riders were a bunch of unwanted rabble rousers whose safety was not his concern. Talking by phone with Kennedy, he claimed that the general who headed the National Guard could not guarantee the protection of King and his church congregation. Kennedy was furious and told Patterson he wanted to speak with the National Guard general. "I want him to say it to me," he thundered. "I want to hear a general of the U.S. Army say he can't protect Martin Luther King, Jr."[9] Patterson finally backed down, and National Guardsmen were ordered to help ensure King and his congregation a safe retreat from the church.

In November 1961, Attorney General Kennedy strongly urged the Interstate Commerce Commission to issue regulations banning segregation on buses and trains, and in terminals and stations. The commission agreed to Kennedy's request. The Justice Department began to enforce these new rules, city by city, and within a year, throughout the South, whites and blacks traveled together on buses and trains and entered terminals and stations that no longer had separate restrooms, water fountains, or other facilities.

The vigorous young attorney general also worked hard to help remove the racial barriers that existed at southern universities and colleges. Although a public institution, the University of Mississippi was one of these schools where no black students were allowed. James Meredith, a black man, wanted to attend "Ole Miss" to complete his studies for a degree in political science. He had served nine years in the U.S. Air Force and had started his college career at Jackson State College, a black school. Although his record showed that he was otherwise qualified for enrollment at the University of Mississippi, his registration was denied because he was black.

The National Association for the Advancement of Colored People (NAACP) then took Meredith's case to court. After two lengthy lawsuits, a judge ruled in Meredith's favor, but enforcement of the court order was blocked by several postponements. Finally, in September 1961, Supreme Court Justice Hugo L. Black ordered that Meredith be admitted to the university.

When Mississippi's governor, Ross Barnett, a fervent believer in the superiority of the white race, was asked whether he would abide by the ruling of Justice Black, he replied defiantly, "Never!" Two days later he went on state television to proclaim, "We will not surrender to the evil and illegal forces of tyranny."[10] Then he announced that all public schools and institutions of higher learning in Mississippi would be controlled by the state government alone and subject only to state laws.

Both the president and the attorney general refused to accept Governor Barnett's edict. Bobby Kennedy had several conversations with Barnett, trying to persuade him to change his point of view, but the governor stubbornly clung to his state's-rights position. The attorney general then sent federal marshals to escort Meredith to the campus at Oxford, Mississippi. Several times Meredith tried to register for classes, but each time he was turned back by mobs of jeering students and local police who threatened him with their clubs. From neighboring areas, cars began crowding into Oxford, driven by irate racists who brought with them various types of weapons. A bloody showdown appeared to be imminent.

Federal forces were hastily assembled to deal with this grave crisis. In addition to the 541 marshals sent to the university campus, the Mississippi National Guard was put into federal service, and combat troops from southern bases were ordered to depart for Oxford. The furious segregationists, numbering in the thousands, attacked the marshals with rocks, stones, iron bars, campus benches, and "Molotov cocktails" (makeshift bombs crudely fashioned from soda bottles filled with gasoline and lit with a rag or paper wick). Even more ominous, here and there the crack of rifles could be heard. Some people in the mob seized a bulldozer from a construction site and tried to ram the sides of a building where they mistakenly thought Meredith was being hidden.

The marshals carried sidearms but were forbidden to use them unless Meredith's life was in immediate danger. They held out as best they could by firing tear gas into the huge crowd. When the regular army contingents arrived in Oxford, they had to fight their way to the campus, and forty of them were hit by missiles or shotgun blasts. The soldiers finally were able to restore peace to the battered area; they arrested more than two hundred members of the unruly mob.

During the fifteen-hour riot, two men were killed; about a third of the marshals—166—were injured; and hundreds of the students and civilians were wounded. The once-beautiful campus was littered with burned and wrecked automobiles, empty tear gas cannisters, broken benches, smashed window glass, and thousands of green, jagged chips from pulverized cola bottles.

The next day James Meredith was enrolled at the university. He attended classes and went to and from the campus under constant guard by federal marshals. Meredith earned his degree and became one of the heroes of the civil rights movement. Later, he traveled to Washington, D.C., and shook hands with the attorney general in his office at the Justice Department. After their meeting, Meredith declared, "The Kennedy Administration, mostly because of

Robert Kennedy, was the first in American history to add moral authority to the black struggle."[11]

In April 1963, after three black students had applied to enter the University of Alabama, George Wallace, the governor of that state, prepared to stand in the doorway of the registrar's office and personally prevent the enrollment of these blacks. Anxious to avoid a repetition of the rioting that had occurred in Mississippi, the attorney general flew to Montgomery to confer with Wallace. The governor firmly insisted that he would never submit voluntarily to any school integration in his state. Kennedy then told him that the Justice Department had to enforce the laws of the land and ensure that court orders were obeyed.

A federal court ruled that the black students must be admitted to the university. But Wallace refused to back down, so Kennedy sent Deputy Attorney General Nicholas Katzenbach and federal marshals to Montgomery. Wallace had ordered that a white line be painted in front of the registration building and, surrounded by state police, warned Katzenbach not to cross that line. The deputy attorney general tried to reason with the governor, but Wallace would not reply.

Katzenbach left the campus and phoned Bobby Kennedy, explaining that Wallace would not comply with the court order to enroll the black students. The attorney general then called the president, who quickly alerted the Alabama National Guard to report for duty under his command. When a brigadier general informed Wallace that the state's National Guard was now under federal control, the governor reluctantly gave up his campaign to keep African-Americans out of the University of Alabama.

As President Kennedy had planned, he turned to Bobby for advice on many subjects, including international problems. Some White House observers called Bobby the "assistant president" because he often influenced the decisions that his older brother had to make. Bobby was at the president's side during that critical period in October 1962 when the United States had to formulate a policy to deal with the missile bases installed by the Soviet Union in Cuba. The military officers who advised the president leaned strongly toward an air strike and even suggested an armed invasion of the island ruled by the Communist dictator Fidel Castro. The attorney general argued strenuously against such action. He pointed out that the United States was still being condemned by other nations for sponsoring the ill-fated invasion of Cuba at the Bay of Pigs in 1961, and he asserted that a full-scale assault against the island "would completely destroy America's moral position in the world."[12] Instead, Bobby Kennedy favored a naval blockade of Cuba by American warships, coupled with a promise not to invade Cuba if the Soviet Union agreed to dismantle its missile bases on the island. This was the policy finally adopted by the president, and it succeeded in resolving the crisis without resort to warfare (see Chapter 5).

When President Kennedy was assassinated in November 1963, Bobby was stunned and deeply saddened. For many weeks after his brother's tragic death, his eyes often moist with tears, he would sit hour after hour staring grimly out of the windows at home and at his office. Gradually he emerged from the depression that had enveloped him. He began to realize that his wife and children needed him and so did the late president's daughter and son, to whom he became virtually a second father. People all across the country urged him to continue working toward the goals that his older brother had set. Many Americans hoped that someday there would be another Kennedy in the White House.

Bobby continued to serve as attorney general for several months in Lyndon B. Johnson's administration. He very much wanted the new president to ask him to run as the Democratic vice presidential nominee in the 1964 election. But personal relations between Johnson and the brother of the slain president, never having been cordial, grew even more strained after JFK's assassination. In July 1964, the president told Bobby that he would not ask the Democratic national convention to select him or any other cabinet member as his running mate. Later, President Johnson announced that Senator Hubert H. Humphrey of Minnesota was his choice for the vice presidential nomination.

Even though his own political future had been blunted, Bobby went to the Democratic national convention because he wanted to introduce a film tribute to his brother Jack. When he walked to the rostrum, the delegates rose to their feet and gave him a resounding ovation that lasted for twenty-two minutes. Although Johnson occupied the White House, it was obvious to a nation watching the convention on television that Robert Kennedy was first in the hearts of many Democrats. To honor the memory of the brother he loved dearly, Bobby quoted this poignant passage from Shakespeare's *Romeo and Juliet*:

> *When he shall die,*
> *Take him and cut him out in little stars,*
> *And he will make the face of Heaven so fine*
> *That all the world will be in love with night,*
> *And pay no worship to the garish sun.*

When Bobby finished his emotional talk, there were few dry eyes in the huge audience. As he left the rostrum, his head was bowed and tears streamed down his face.

Later that same year, Bobby resigned from his position as attorney general. He established a residence in New York and ran for the Senate from that state. Since he had been living at Hickory Hill in Virginia, some New Yorkers called Bobby a carpetbagger who had come to their state simply to promote his own political self-interest. But many other voters eagerly flocked to his banner. Enormous cheering crowds greeted him wherever he spoke. His candor, his idealism, and his genuine compassion for society's underdogs—the people who had to endure poverty and injustice—made him very popular, especially among minorities and young voters. In November 1964, he unseated his Republican opponent, Senator Kenneth Keating, winning by a margin of nearly 720,000 votes.

As a senator, Bobby became increasingly involved in the struggles of poor people and minority groups. Together with New York's other senator, the liberal Republican Jacob Javits, he sponsored an amendment to the Aid-to-Appalachia Bill that added thirty-three counties in New York State to the number of poverty-stricken areas that were to receive federal funds. He and Javits also sponsored a bill that gave the vote to non-English-speaking Puerto Ricans if they could pass a literacy test in another language. Once this bill became a law, many Puerto Ricans living in New York and other states gained full citizenship rights for the first time. Senator Kennedy, enlisting the aid of business and community leaders, helped launch a massive project that brought major improvements to the Bedford-Stuyvesant section of Brooklyn, New York, which had been one of the most depressed black slums in the nation. Kennedy strove to better the conditions of the poor farm workers, mainly Mexican-Americans, in California and the Native Americans who lived on reservations. Bobby's activities were widely covered in the news, and before the end of 1966 both the Gallup and Harris polls reported that he was more popular than President Johnson among Democratic and independent voters.

The chief reason for Johnson's declining popularity was his determined effort to escalate the Vietnam War, a policy that did not meet with the approval of a growing number of people in the United States. In 1966, almost 400,000 members of the American armed forces were engaged in the conflict, and continuous bombing of North Vietnam had failed to produce any sign of a Communist surrender. When his brother had been president, Bobby had favored the small, limited role of the United States in the war. But as American participation on Asian battlefields greatly expanded under President Johnson—and the number of American casualties steadily mounted—Kennedy became an outspoken critic of the president's stubborn commitment to the war. Both in the Senate and on speaking tours, Bobby called for the United States to pull out of the war that he felt could not be won and begin the difficult process of reuniting a badly divided nation that had been torn apart by the friction between antiwar protesters and those who supported Johnson's military campaign.

Some prominent leaders of the antiwar movement encouraged the senator from New York to run against Johnson for the Democratic presidential nomination in the 1968 election. But Bobby, knowing it was very difficult to prevent an incumbent president from winning his own party's nomination for reelection, at first declined to become a candidate. Then something happened on March 12, 1968, that caused him to change his mind. In the nation's first Democratic primary election in New Hampshire, Senator Eugene McCarthy of Minnesota, an ardent opponent of the Vietnam War, won an astonishing 42 percent of the vote against Johnson's 49 percent, and McCarthy captured twenty of the state's twenty-four delegates. The strong antiwar sentiment demonstrated by the New Hampshire voters brought Robert Kennedy into the race on March 16. Two weeks later, on March 31, President Johnson stunned the nation by announcing that he would not run for another term. Most of his supporters then switched their allegiance to Vice President Hubert Humphrey, who entered the contest in April. Since he did not run in any state primary elections, Humphrey based his candidacy on the backing he expected to receive from party chieftains and state organizations.

McCarthy and Kennedy battled each other in five primaries in the states of Indiana, Nebraska, Oregon, South Dakota, and California. Kennedy won impressive victories in Indiana and Nebraska, but on May 28 his campaign temporarily stalled in Oregon, which McCarthy carried by a vote of 44 percent to 38 percent. Attention then shifted to California, with its large number of delegates. Both candidates fought hard for the California vote, knowing that whoever won in that state would have a good chance to gain the Democratic presidential nomination and to capture the White House in November.

On June 4, the day of the California and South Dakota primary elections, Kennedy was in Los Angeles. At his headquarters in the Ambassador Hotel, he learned early in the evening that he had carried South Dakota decisively. The polls in California did not close until eight o'clock, so both the Kennedy and McCarthy camps waited nervously as the votes from that all-important state were counted. Shortly after eleven o'clock, it became apparent that Kennedy had won the California primary (the final results gave him 46.3 percent of the vote to McCarthy's 41.8 percent). Just before he went from his hotel suite to the ballroom where his jubilant supporters were waiting to greet him, Bobby said to his close friend, Kenneth O'Donnell, "You know, Kenny, I feel now for the first time that I've shaken off the shadow of my brother. I feel I made it on my own."[13]

Kennedy knew now that McCarthy's candidacy had finally been crushed and that his only remaining rival for the presidential nomination was Vice President Humphrey. When he addressed the cheering throng in the hotel ballroom, he proposed to debate the vice president on crucial problems, such as ". . . What we are going to do with those who still suffer within the United States from hunger . . . and whether we're going to continue the policies that have been so unsuccessful in Vietnam—of American troops and American Marines carrying the major burden of that conflict. I do not want this and I think we can move in a different direction."[14]

Moments later, his speech completed, Bobby retreated through a dimly lit kitchen corridor to avoid being mobbed by enthusiastic well-wishers. Behind a food tray rack crouched an armed assassin. As the senator approached, Sirhan Sirhan, a young Palestinian Arab, stepped forward and raised his .22 caliber revolver to within an inch of Bobby's head. He fired a bullet that tore through the right mastoid bone and lodged in Kennedy's brain. Two more shots struck the senator's right armpit as he tumbled to the floor. Sirhan continued firing, wounding five other persons before he was wrestled onto a steel steam table by Kennedy's friends.

Bobby Kennedy was rushed to a hospital, but his wounds were fatal. He died twenty-five hours after he was shot, at the age of forty-two. His body was flown to New York City, where his funeral was conducted at St. Patrick's Cathedral and televised to a mourning nation. In a spontaneous outpouring of emotion usually reserved for fallen presidents, thousands of solemn viewers lined the tracks as a train carried him on his final journey to the nation's capital. Bobby was buried in Arlington National Cemetery near the grave of his brother Jack.

Sirhan told the police that he had committed this terrible crime for his Arab brothers and arrogantly said that Kennedy got what was coming to him. The Palestinian's deep-seated hatred for his victim apparently stemmed from Bobby's well-known support for Israel and the Jewish people. Sirhan was convicted and sentenced to death in the gas chamber, but his sentence was later reduced to life imprisonment when the Supreme Court ruled in 1972 that the death penalty was unconstitutional.

Hubert Humphrey won the 1968 Democratic presidential nomination at a convention that was marred by ugly street fighting between the Chicago police and various groups of antiwar protesters. The Republican party nominated former Vice President Richard Nixon as its presidential candidate, and Nixon barely defeated Humphrey in a very close contest.

President Nixon began withdrawing some American troops from Vietnam in July 1969, but U.S. ground forces were caught in severe fighting as late as 1972. Heavy air raids on North Vietnam were ordered in March 1970 and again in November 1972. The withdrawal of the last American troops from Vietnam did not occur until 1973, more than four years after Nixon had assumed the presidency.

Moreover, President Nixon in 1970 enlarged the Asiatic war by ordering a military strike against Cambodia, Vietnam's neighbor, in an effort to destroy enemy sanctuaries near the border, disrupt supply lines, and support non-Communist armies in a civil war against Cambodian Communists. This military campaign in Cambodia, kept secret at first, failed to produce the desired results. But it drew a rising storm of protest in the United States, most dramatically on the campus of Kent State University, where Ohio National Guardsmen drew their guns and fired into a crowd of demonstrators, killing four and wounding nine.

Had Robert Kennedy lived, there is a strong possibility that he would have won the presidency in 1968. Undoubtedly he would have had much stronger support than Humphrey did among antiwar protesters, and his name on the ballot probably would have drawn to the polls a higher percentage of blacks, Hispanic-Americans, and poor people in both urban and rural areas. If he had become president, he almost certainly would have brought a much swifter end to the participation of the United States in the Vietnam War, and it is extremely doubtful that he would have committed American forces to warfare in Cambodia.

After his death, many people paid tribute to Bobby and praised his accomplishments in both the Justice Department and the Senate. His only living brother, Senator Edward Kennedy of Massachusetts, said, "He should be remembered simply as a good and decent man who saw wrong and tried to right it, saw suffering and tried to heal it, saw war and tried to stop it."[15]

NOTES

CHAPTER ONE

1. Jim Bishop, *The Day Lincoln Was Shot* (New York: Harper & Row, 1955), 53.
2. Page Smith, *Trial by Fire* (New York: McGraw-Hill, 1982), 522.
3. Ibid.
4. Oscar Handlin and Lilian Handlin, *Abraham Lincoln and the Union* (Boston: Little, Brown, 1980), 184.
5. Smith, *Trial*, 586.
6. Bishop, *Day Lincoln Was Shot*, 105.
7. Ibid.
8. Smith, *Trial*, 579.
9. Richard W. Murphy, *The Nation Reunited: War's Aftermath* (New York: Time-Life Books, 1987), 20.
10. Ibid., 16.
11. Ibid., 40.
12. Thomas A. Bailey and David M. Kennedy, *The American Pageant* (Lexington, Mass.: D. C. Heath, 1979), 423.

CHAPTER TWO

1. Margaret Leech and Harry J. Brown, *The Garfield Orbit* (New York: Harper & Row, 1978), 203–4.

2. Bill Severn, *Teacher, Soldier, President: The Life of James A. Garfield* (New York: Ives Washburn, 1964), 145.
3. Leech and Brown, *Garfield Orbit*, 209.
4. Severn, *Teacher, Soldier*, 148.
5. *Presidential Elections Since 1789* (Washington, D.C.: Congressional Quarterly Inc., 1979), 78.
6. Severn, *Teacher, Soldier*, 122.
7. Leech and Brown, *Garfield Orbit*, 160.
8. Severn, *Teacher, Soldier*, 157.
9. James W. Clarke, *American Assassins: The Darker Side of Politics* (Princeton, N.J.: Princeton Unviersity Press, 1982), 206.
10. Ibid., 207.
11. Leech and Brown, *Garfield Orbit*, 244.
12. George F. Howe, *Chester A. Arthur: A Quarter-Century of Machine Politics* (New York: Frederick Ungar, 1957), 151.
13. Ibid., 254.

CHAPTER THREE

1. Margaret Leech, *In the Days of McKinley* (New York: Harper & Brothers, 1959), 23.
2. Eugene H. Roseboom and Alfred E. Eckles, Jr., *A History of Presidential Elections from George Washington to Jimmy Carter* (New York: Macmillan, 1979), 121.
3. Paul F. Boller, Jr., *Presidential Campaigns* (New York: Oxford University Press, 1984), 180.
4. James W. Clarke, *American Assassins: The Darker Side of Politics* (Princeton, N.J.: Princeton University Press, 1982), 58.
5. Ibid., 59.
6. John Mason Potter, *Plots against the President* (New York: Astor-Honor, 1968), 172.
7. *The American Heritage Pictorial History of the Presidents of the United States* (New York: American Heritage, 1968), 2:629.

CHAPTER FOUR

1. Arthur M. Schlesinger, Jr., *The Politics of Upheaval* (Boston: Houghton Mifflin, 1960), 43.
2. Ibid., 47.
3. Alan Brinkley, *Voices of Protest: Huey Long, Father Coughlin, and the Great Depression* (New York: Knopf, 1982), 26.
4. T. Harry Williams, *Huey Long* (New York: Knopf, 1970), 7.
5. Ibid.
6. Brinkley, *Voices of Protest*, 79–80.
7. Edmund Lindop, *The Turbulent Thirties* (New York: Watts, 1970), 40.
8. Williams, *Huey Long*, 8.

CHAPTER FIVE

1. William Manchester, *One Brief Shining Moment: Remembering Kennedy* (Boston: Little, Brown, 1983), 10.
2. Eugene H. Roseboom and Alfred E. Eckles, Jr., *A History of Presidential Elections from George Washington to Jimmy Carter* (New York: Macmillan, 1979), 255.
3. Michael Barone, *Our Country: The Shaping of America from Roosevelt to Reagan* (New York: Macmillan, 1990), 336.
4. William Manchester, *The Glory and the Dream: A Narrative History of America, 1932–1972* (Boston: Little, Brown, 1974), 2:1091.
5. Barone, *Our Country*, 336.
6. Manchester, *One Brief Shining Moment*, 207.
7. Barone, *Our Country*, 346.
8. Manchester, *Glory and the Dream*, 2:1190.
9. Manchester, *One Brief Shining Moment*, 227.
10. James MacGregor Burns, *The Crosswinds of Freedom* (New York: Knopf, 1989), 370.
11. I. E. Levine, *Young Man in the White House: John Fitzgerald Kennedy* (New York: Messner, 1964), 178.
12. Manchester, *One Brief Shining Moment*, 21.
13. *The Warren Report: The Official Report on the Assassination of President John F. Kennedy* (New York: Associated Press, 1964), 21.
14. Manchester, *One Brief Shining Moment*, 224–25.
15. Ibid.
16. Levine, *Young Man*, 176.

CHAPTER SIX

1. Flip Schulke and Penelope McPhee, *King Remembered* (New York: Pocket Books, 1986), 20–21.
2. Edmund Lindop, *An Album of the Fifties* (New York: Watts, 1978), 54.
3. James MacGregor Burns, *The Crosswinds of Freedom* (New York: Knopf, 1989), 348–49.
4. Nancy Shuker, *Martin Luther King* (New York: Chelsea House, 1985), 53.
5. Jim Bishop, *The Days of Martin Luther King, Jr.* (New York: Putnam's, 1971), 157.
6. Schulke and McPhee, *King Remembered*, 49–60.
7. Burns, *Crosswinds*, 360.
8. Ibid., 367–68.
9. Shuker, *Martin Luther King*, 18–19.
10. James Haskins, *The Life and Death of Martin Luther King, Jr.* (New York: Lothrop, Lee & Shepard, 1977), 92.
11. William Manchester, *The Glory and the Dream: A Narrative History of America, 1932–1972* (Boston: Little, Brown, 1974), 2:1383.

12. James W. Clarke, *American Assassins: The Darker Side of Politics* (Princeton, N.J.: Princeton University Press, 1982), 239–57.

CHAPTER SEVEN

1. Theodore C. Sorenson, *The Kennedy Legacy* (New York: Macmillan, 1969), 34–35.
2. Charles P. Graves, *Robert F. Kennedy: Man Who Dared to Dream* (Champaign, Ill.: Garrard, 1970), 29.
3. Edmund Lindop and Joseph Jares, *White House Sportsmen* (Boston: Houghton Mifflin, 1964), 14.
4. Gene Schoor, *Young Robert Kennedy* (New York: McGraw-Hill, 1969), 111.
5. Arthur M. Schlesinger, Jr., *Robert Kennedy and His Times* (New York: Ballantine, 1978), 102.
6. Richard J. Whalen, *The Founding Father: The Story of Joseph P. Kennedy* (New York: New American Library, 1964), 421.
7. Lester David and Irene David, *Bobby Kennedy: The Making of a Folk Hero* (New York: Dodd, Mead, 1986), 69–70.
8. Graves, *Robert F. Kennedy*, 48–49.
9. Flip Schulke and Penelope McPhee, *King Remembered* (New York: Pocket Books, 1986), 107.
10. William Manchester, *The Glory and the Dream: A Narrative History of America, 1932–1972* (Boston: Little, Brown, 1974), 2:1157.
11. David and David, *Bobby Kennedy*, 211.
12. Arthur M. Schlesinger, Jr., ed., *The Alamanac of American History* (New York: Putnam's, 1983), 562.
13. David and David, *Bobby Kennedy*, 316.
14. Jules Witcover, *85 Days: The Last Campaign of Robert Kennedy* (New York: Morrow, 1988), 264.
15. Graves, *Robert F. Kennedy*, 95.

FOR FURTHER
READING

Barone, Michael. *Our Country: The Shaping of America from Roosevelt to Reagan.* New York: Macmillan, 1990.

Bishop, Jim. *The Day Lincoln Was Shot.* New York: Harper & Row, 1955.

Brinkley, Alan. *Voices of Protest: Huey Long, Father Coughlin, and the Great Depression.* New York: Knopf, 1982.

Burns, James MacGregor. *The Crosswinds of Freedom.* New York: Knopf, 1989.

Clarke, James W. *American Assassins: The Darker Side of Politics.* Princeton, N.J.: Princeton University Press, 1982.

David, Lester, and Irene David. *Bobby Kennedy: The Making of a Folk Hero.* New York: Dodd, Mead, 1986.

Donovan, Robert J. *The Assassins.* New York: Harper & Row, 1955.

Goode, Stephen. *Assassination! Kennedy, King, Kennedy.* New York: Watts, 1979.

Graves, Charles P. *Robert Kennedy: Man Who Dared to Dream.* Champaign, Ill.: Garrard, 1970.

Handlin, Oscar, and Lilian Handlin. *Abraham Lincoln and the Union.* Boston: Little, Brown, 1980.

Haskins, James. *The Life and Death of Martin Luther King, Jr.* New York: Lothrop, Lee & Shepard, 1977.

Howe, George F. *Chester A. Arthur: A Quarter-Century of Machine Politics.* New York: Frederick Ungar, 1964.

Katz, William. *An Album of Reconstruction.* New York: Watts, 1974.

Leech, Margaret, and Harry J. Brown. *The Garfield Orbit.* New York: Harper & Row, 1978.

———. *In the Days of McKinley.* New York: Harper & Brothers, 1959.

Lesberg, Sandy. *Assassins in Our Time.* London: Peebles Press, 1976.

Levine, I. E. *Young Man in the White House: John Fitzgerald Kennedy.* New York: Messner, 1964

McKinley, James. *Assassination in America.* New York: Harper & Row, 1977.

Manchester, William. *One Brief Shining Moment: Remembering Kennedy.* Boston: Little, Brown, 1983.

Murphy, Richard W. *The Nation Reunited: War's Aftermath.* New York: Time-Life Books, 1987.

Potter, John Mason. *Plots against the President.* New York: Astor-Honor, 1968.

Schlesinger, Arthur M., Jr. *Robert Kennedy and His Times.* New York: Ballantine, 1978.

———. *The Politics of Upheaval.* Boston: Houghton Mifflin, 1960.

Schulke, Flip, and Penelope McPhee. *King Remembered.* New York: Pocket Books, 1986.

Severn, Bill. *Teacher, Soldier, President: The Life of James A. Garfield.* New York: Ives, Washburn, 1964.

Shuker, Nancy. *Martin Luther King.* New York: Chelsea House, 1985.

Williams, T. Harry. *Huey Long.* New York: Knopf, 1970.

INDEX

137

A B O U T   T H E
A U T H O R

More than one million copies of books by Edmund Lindop have been sold. He has written eight Watts books, including *Presidents by Accident* and *The Bill of Rights and Landmark Cases*. For many years Mr. Lindop taught history and government classes at University High School in Los Angeles and helped train new teachers for the University of Southern California and the University of California, Los Angeles.